Text

11-14

Connections

Bernadette Carroll
Melinda Derry
Maria Moran
Denise Savage
Nisha Tank

PEARSON
Longman

Series editor: Bernadette Carroll

Contents

Contents

Introduction

Reading is an important skill. Texts are everywhere and by developing your ability in reading you can unlock hidden meanings and build up a greater understanding of the world around you. Improving your reading can also lead to improvements in your speaking and listening and writing skills, so it is a vital skill.

Text Connections 11–14 contains 16 units. Each unit has a different theme and contains three linked texts. You will learn how to use a wide range of reading strategies to help you to understand these texts better. Let's take a closer look at the structure of a unit.

1	**Title and introduction**	After the title of the unit, which tells you the theme, the first thing you'll see is an introduction. Don't ignore this! It gives you background information explaining the theme and a few hints about the texts in the unit.
2	**List of texts**	The three texts are listed across the page. You might want to have a quick look at each text if the title isn't enough of a clue.
3	**Reading strategies**	Next is a list of the reading strategies you will be using during the unit. Look them up on pages 7–8 if you need to remind yourself what they mean.
4	**Pre-reading activity**	Then there is a pre-reading activity. This focuses on one of the reading strategies and prepares you for the reading of the texts themselves.
5	**Text: introduction and activities**	For each text, you then have an introduction to that particular text, the text itself and a sequence of activities. As shown in the contents (pages 2–5), the activities are linked to the Assessment Focuses you will meet when you take your national tests. Take note of these because they are a clue about the sort of answer that the question is looking for.
6	**Compare task**	The unit ends with a compare task. This means you are going to explore a common focus in two or more of the texts. The work you have done in the other activities should have prepared you for this final task.

As well as using the reading strategies on pages 7–8, you will also use four different types of reading: skimming, scanning, close reading and continuous reading. Look at the information on the next page to find out when and how to use these different types of reading.

Types of reading

Skimming

When?
- When you need only a general idea of what the text is about.
- When you need to check that the text is going to be useful. When you are trying to get an initial understanding of the text.

How?
- Run your eyes quickly over the text.
- Look at headlines, headings, subheadings, titles, the opening lines of paragraphs and words that signal a new point is being made.

Scanning

When?
- When you want to find a specific piece of information quickly.

How?
- Quickly glance down the text for key words.
- Run your finger down the middle of the page as you read to focus your eyes and keep them moving.
- Keep a visual picture in your head of key words that you are looking for.

Close reading

When?
- When you need to explore the details in the text.

How?
- Read all the words in a short section.
- Read and re-read difficult sections, revising your interpretations each time.
- Use text-marking to identify key points and paraphrase what the writer is saying.

Continuous reading

When?
- When reading for pleasure or to understand a full account of something.

How?
- Read all of the words, but you might be able to read some sections very quickly.
- Others might need a slower pace to let you take in all of the ideas.

Reading strategies

Good readers use a range of reading strategies to help them get the most out of their reading. Refer to this list as you work through the book to remind you of the strategies you need to use.

See images
- Visualise what the writer is describing. What pictures can you see of the characters, the settings and the action?
- Ask others about their mental pictures and tell them about yours. Are they the same?

Hear a reading voice
- As you read, think about whose voice you are hearing and how it changes.
- Think about how the central characters sound and the sound effects of all the action. What can you hear while you read?

Establish a relationship with the narrator
- Think about the narrator – the person telling you the information in the text. Identify who the narrator is. Do you like her/him? What would you say to her/him if she/he were in the room now?

Establish a relationship with the writer
- Can you hear the writer's voice? Is the author hiding behind a narrator or character or speaking directly to the reader?
- What do you think the writer is trying to say to you?

Predict what will happen
- Weather forecasts use facts and prior knowledge to predict the weather. Use what you know about a text to suggest what you think will happen next.
- Can you explain why? What evidence have you got?

Speculate
- Gaze into that crystal ball! What do you see? What do you think could happen in the end? Think of different possibilities.
- Discuss your speculations with others.

Ask questions

- Ask yourself questions all the time: who, why, what, where, when, how? Why do the characters do what they do? Why did that event happen and why did it happen in that way?
- Ask yourself why the writer has written the text in this way. What is the significance of the details the author includes? Do the details mean something?

Make judgements

- What do you **really** think? Share your opinion of the characters, the settings and the events with others. Do you like them? If not, why not? Did your opinions change as you read more?

Rationalise what is happening

- Step outside the text and look on the events as a detached observer, like a reporter.
- Think logically about the characters or people, what they do and what happens to them. Does everything make sense? If not, why not?

Feel

- Try and feel what the characters or people are feeling in the situation that they are in. What do you want to happen to them?
- What feelings does the writer want you to have about the characters and what is happening?

Empathise

- Imagine you are in the same situation as the characters or people. What would you do? How would you feel?

Reinterpret

- As you read, consider how your ideas about the people and events in the text are changing.
- Do you feel and think the same as you did at the beginning? With more information your reaction might now be different.

Interpret patterns

- Think about how the characters are linked. What are the similarities and differences between them? Can you group some of them together? And if so, what does each group represent?
- Think about how the events are linked. Are they random or are they leading somewhere in particular?

Relate to your own experience

- Does this remind you of anything you have done in your life or anything you have seen or heard about?
- How does this make you feel about the events in the text?

Relate to previous reading experience

- Compare what you are reading with other texts that you have read. In what ways is it similar or different?
- What features of this type of text do you recognise or expect to see?

Infer

- Look for what is being implied rather than made explicit. Read between the lines to find the meaning.
- The choice of words and how they are organised are ways writers can suggest different meanings.

Deduce

- Be a detective. Use evidence in the text to work out what is meant. You might have to fill some gaps and make links between ideas.

Read backwards and forwards

- Think of this as a chance to rewind and fast-forward. Clarify your understanding by making links back to what you have just read and forward to what is coming next.

Re-read

- Can you spot anything new that you didn't see before?
- Try to deepen your understanding as you become more familiar with the text.

1 Growing up

Introduction

We all go through several changes as we grow up from a child to a teenager. Often we start to question things that we have always accepted. Our tastes and interests usually alter and we may try out new beliefs and friendships. It can be difficult coming to terms with the changes in our feelings. We can become confused and vulnerable to many influences, so it is important to be able to answer the question 'Who am I?'

 The first week   What sort of person are you?   A country childhood

Reading strategies

- hear a reading voice
- infer
- relate to your own experience
- empathise
- make judgements
- deduce

Pre-reading: relate to your own experience

1 When we read, it is often helpful to relate the ideas in the text to our own experiences. With a partner, list some of the things that interested you when you were younger that no longer hold any interest for you. You might like to consider some of the following:

- hobbies and interests
- clothes
- music
- food
- television
- games and toys
- family events
- beliefs
- attitudes
- anything else you can think of.

Choose four of these categories and write two examples for each.

2 Compare your list with another pair. Try to establish the two or three most important changes you have all made. Are there any similarities or differences?

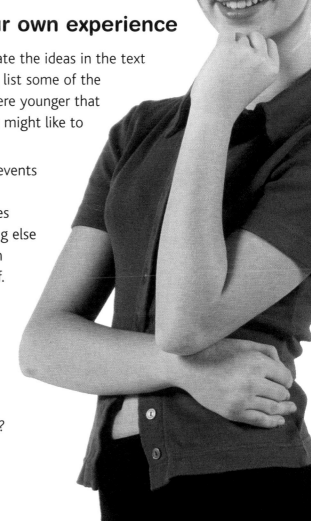

Growing up

Arriving at a new school can be a very scary experience. You have to get used to new rules, new systems, new teachers and new friends. We all want to be accepted, but making new friends can be a tricky business! This text is taken from an information book, *Staying Cool, Surviving School*, and offers advice about making friends.

The first week

Making friends

This is what everyone dreads. 'Supposing no-one talks to me' is the worst worry of all as the school bus draws up at the bus stop. With a bit of luck some of your primary school friends will be going to the same school so there will be a few familiar faces. While it is terribly tempting to stick like limpets to people you know, and quite okay to do so for the first couple of days, it's a good idea to get to know other people as well. But to do this with any degree of success you need to observe a while. There are a lot of telltale signs that will help you pick out those you want to cultivate[1] and those best avoided.

The Queen Bees (or King Pins)

'Well, hi there, I'm Stella, who are you?' This is a typical introduction from the Potential Leader of the Pack, the sort of embryo PR type who has no qualms[2] about anything – or so it seems. Oozing self-confidence from every pore, they purport to know everything about everybody and far from exhibiting first-day nerves, usually end up as Class Prefect, Person in Charge of Library Tickets and Producer of the Class Play by the middle of the first week. The male variety, the King Pins, are somewhat more aggressive. They will assure anyone with the time and inclination to listen that they are going to carve a path through the school, make people sit up and take notice and change anything they don't like.

WARNING: Queen Bees and King Pins tend to ditch anyone who is not prepared to worship at their throne, or dares to suggest that their way is not necessarily the best. In short, they are only happy when they are the centre of attention and may well use other people for their own ends. Handle with care.

The Bullies

These are the worst type of kid anywhere. They use their own strength to play on other people's weaknesses and can make the lives of their victims sheer hell. Basically they are cowards who can only feel at ease with themselves when they are making someone else's life a misery. There is never any good reason for bullying. If you ever see anyone being bullied, make it your business to tell someone in authority at once.

[1]cultivate – *develop*   [2]qualms – *worries*

Not tomorrow, not later today. NOW. Tomorrow may be too late.

If it is *you* that is being bullied, you must also tell someone at once. The bullies may say they will get you for it, but they won't be allowed to if you go straight to the top. Tell the Head, tell your class teacher, tell the police if necessary. But don't let them get a hold over you. If you want more advice, read *Don't Pick On Me* (Piccadilly Press, £5.99) – it's a great book and stops you feeling that no-one out there understands. But DO something. Your life and your peace of mind are too precious to be threatened by anyone.

The Cool Trendies

These are the guys and girls who wear the hip outfits with that certain style that is always The Look of the Moment. Never mind *in* fashion; they *make* the fashion. They are totally on top of every situation, set the trends for the rest of the school and appear to lick every problem into place by breaktime. You are bound to envy them but don't; the trouble with their lifestyle is that it is very transient. They have to keep thinking up new scams to keep ahead. Exhausting.

The majority

Having listed all the quirks of kids above, you may wonder if you will find anyone just like you. In fact, the vast majority are thoroughly ordinary, normal everyday types who have their good days, bad days and bored days. Whatever you may think as you stand, knees-a-tremble, in line for your first Assembly, they all have their worries as well, be they difficult parents, BO or sticking out teeth. Give them all a chance and you will end up with a whole clutch of new friends.

From *Staying Cool, Surviving School* by Rosie Rushton

Explaining the ideas

1   Working in pairs, scan the text and **infer** the disadvantages of befriending the Queen Bees and King Pins, the Bullies and the Cool Trendies. Present these as a series of bullet points using your own words.

Queen Bees/King Pins	The Bullies	The Cool Trendies
• They ditch anyone not prepared to worship them	• Pick on people's weaknesses	• Have to be fashionable
•	•	•
•	•	•

2   Close read the sections 'Making friends' and 'The majority'.

   a   List the advice that is given in these two sections about making friends at school.

   b   Turn the advice into a series of 'Dos and Don'ts' about friendship. You could turn this into a poster that could be displayed in classrooms. **Make judgements** about the important advice to include on the poster.

11

Text 2 Growing up

When you are a teenager, your physical body changes as you turn into an adult. However, your thoughts and feelings are changing as well and you may experience mood swings with highs and lows. It is therefore important to remain positive, to find out 'who you are' and to try to feel good about yourself, as the following text explains.

WHAT SORT OF PERSON ARE YOU?

When you're feeling especially confused about who you are, it might be a good time to ask yourself a few simple questions.

1 What do you most like about yourself?

2 What makes you happiest?

3 What pleases you?

4 What makes you angry?

5 What excites you?

6 What bores you?

7 How do you like to spend your spare time?

Some questions are a little more complicated. For instance, a group of friends may be talking about a television programme which they all enjoy. Do you agree with them because you genuinely enjoy the programme too, or because you don't want to be different? Do you even disagree just to be contrary or to draw attention to yourself?

Answering these questions honestly can be hard. But there is no point in fooling yourself. Finding out what you think enables you to establish your own individual points of view. As you grow to know yourself better, you will also discover your limitations. You could make a list of all the things you'd like to do in your life. You'll realize that there are probably some things that you cannot do and will never do. Coming to terms with this is particularly important. But remember, it's up to you to choose what you want out of life. It's up to you to decide whether or not you develop your own special talents.

From *Growing Up*
(Merlion publishing)

Explaining the ideas

1 a Scan the first paragraph. What advice is given for when you feel confused about who you are?

b Which two questions in the numbered list would you find the most difficult to answer? Why? **Relate to your own experiences.**

c Close read the third paragraph at the top of the right-hand column. Explain in your own words why some questions are more complicated to answer. Can you **relate this to your own experience**?

d Now close read the last paragraph. Give two reasons why it helps to find out for yourself what you are really like.

e Write down three bullet points that summarise what this article is about.

Looking at language

2 How does this article try to appeal to young people? Try to **hear a reading voice** and think about the following features:

- the use of pronouns
- the type of punctuation used
- the 'voice' of the writer
- the type of advice given.

For each feature, pick out an example from the text and then explain what effect it has on the reader.

Growing up

Nelson Mandela spent 26 years of his life in prison for his political beliefs. He is now a much-admired and influential political figure, travelling all around the world. Yet he was born in a small village in rural South Africa and, from an early age, learned the traditions, beliefs and ways of his ancestors. This text is an extract from his autobiography, *Long Walk to Freedom*, and describes his childhood experiences.

A country childhood

My mother presided over three huts at Qunu[1] which, as I remember, were always filled with the babies and children of my relations. In fact, I hardly recall any occasion as a child when I was alone. In African culture, the sons and daughters of one's aunts or uncles are considered brothers and sisters, not cousins.

Of my mother's three huts, one was used for cooking, one for sleeping and one for storage. In the hut in which we slept, there was no furniture in the Western sense. We slept on mats and sat on the ground. My mother cooked food in a three-legged iron pot over an open fire in the centre of the hut or outside. Everything we ate we grew and made ourselves.

From an early age, I spent most of my free time in the veld[2] playing and fighting with the other boys of the village. A boy who remained at home tied to his mother's apron strings was regarded as a sissy. At night, I shared my food and blanket with these same boys. I was no more than five when I became a herd-boy looking after sheep and calves in the fields. It was in the fields that I learned how to knock birds out of the sky with a slingshot, to gather wild honey and fruits and edible roots, to drink warm, sweet milk straight from the udder of a cow, to swim in the clear, cold streams, and to catch fish with twine and sharpened bits of wire. I learned to stick-fight – essential knowledge to any rural African boy – and became adept at its various techniques, parrying blows, feinting in one direction and striking in another, breaking away from an opponent with quick footwork. From these days I date my love of the veld, of open spaces, the simple beauties of nature, the clean line of the horizon.

[1]Qunu – *a small village in South Africa*   [2]veld – *grassland*

As boys, we were mostly left to our own devices. We played with toys we made ourselves. We moulded animals and birds out of clay. We made ox-drawn sledges out of tree branches. Nature was our playground. The hills above Qunu were dotted with large smooth rocks which we transformed into our own roller-coaster. We sat on flat stones and slid down the face of the large rocks. We did this until our backsides were so sore we could hardly sit down. I learned to ride by sitting atop weaned calves – after being thrown to the ground several times, one got the hang of it.

I learned my lesson one day from an unruly donkey. We had been taking turns climbing up and down its back and when my chance came I jumped on and the donkey bolted into a nearby thornbush. It bent its head, trying to unseat me, which it did, but not before the thorns had pricked and scratched my face, embarrassing me in front of my friends. Like the people of the East, Africans have a highly developed sense of dignity, or what the Chinese call 'face'. I had lost face among my friends. Even though it was a donkey that unseated me, I learned to humiliate another person is to make him suffer an unnecessarily cruel fate. Even as a boy, I defeated my opponents without dishonouring them.

Usually the boys played among themselves, but we sometimes allowed our sisters to join us. Boys and girls would play games like *ndize* (hide and seek) and *icekwa* (tag). But the game I most enjoyed playing with the girls was what we called *khetha*, or choose-the-one-you-like. This was not so much an organized game, but a spur-of-the-moment sport that took place when we accosted a group of girls our own age and demanded that each select the boy she loved. Our rules dictated that the girl's choice be respected and once she had chosen her favourite, she was free to continue on her journey escorted by the lucky boy she loved. But the girls were nimble-witted – far cleverer than we doltish[3] lads – and would often confer among themselves and choose one boy, usually the plainest fellow, and then tease him all the way home.

The most popular game for boys was *thinti*, and like most boys' games it was a youthful approximation of war. Two sticks, used as targets, would be driven firmly into the ground in an upright position about a hundred feet apart. The goal of the game was for each team to hurl sticks at the opposing target and knock it down. We each defended our own target and attempted to prevent the other side from retrieving the sticks that had been thrown over. As we grew older, we organized matches against boys from neighbouring villages and those who distinguished themselves in these fraternal[4] battles were greatly admired, as generals who achieve great victories in war are justly celebrated.

[3]doltish – *silly*   [4]fraternal – *brotherly*

continued ▶

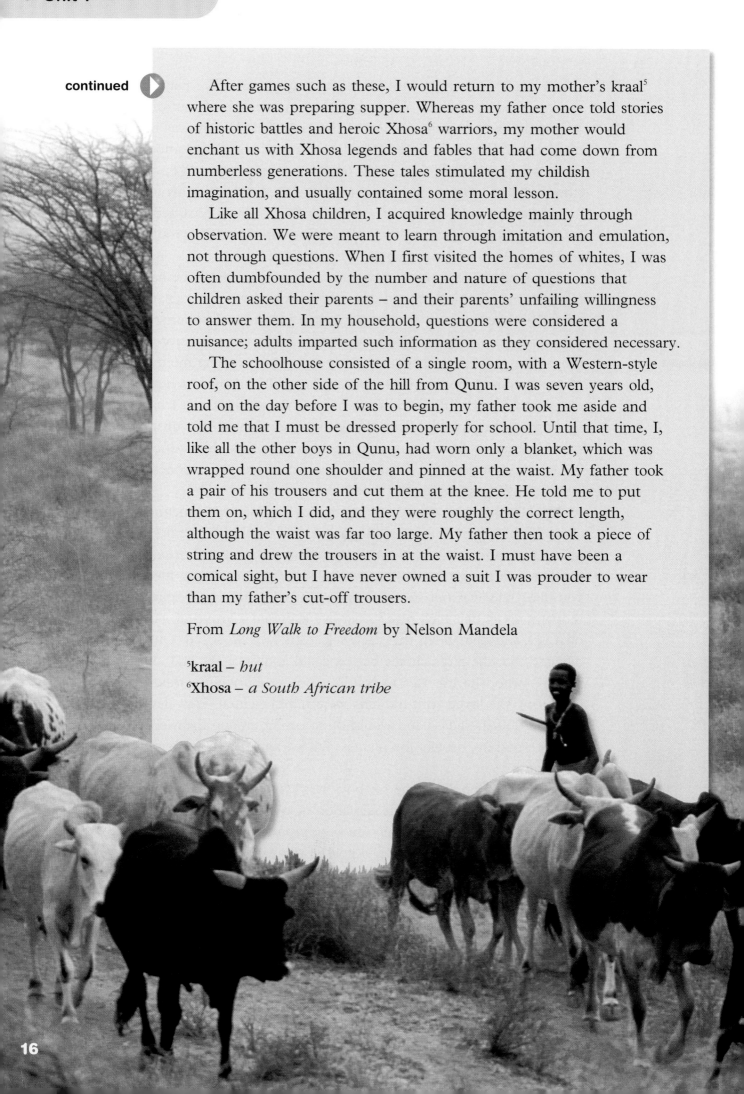

continued

After games such as these, I would return to my mother's kraal[5] where she was preparing supper. Whereas my father once told stories of historic battles and heroic Xhosa[6] warriors, my mother would enchant us with Xhosa legends and fables that had come down from numberless generations. These tales stimulated my childish imagination, and usually contained some moral lesson.

Like all Xhosa children, I acquired knowledge mainly through observation. We were meant to learn through imitation and emulation, not through questions. When I first visited the homes of whites, I was often dumbfounded by the number and nature of questions that children asked their parents – and their parents' unfailing willingness to answer them. In my household, questions were considered a nuisance; adults imparted such information as they considered necessary.

The schoolhouse consisted of a single room, with a Western-style roof, on the other side of the hill from Qunu. I was seven years old, and on the day before I was to begin, my father took me aside and told me that I must be dressed properly for school. Until that time, I, like all the other boys in Qunu, had worn only a blanket, which was wrapped round one shoulder and pinned at the waist. My father took a pair of his trousers and cut them at the knee. He told me to put them on, which I did, and they were roughly the correct length, although the waist was far too large. My father then took a piece of string and drew the trousers in at the waist. I must have been a comical sight, but I have never owned a suit I was prouder to wear than my father's cut-off trousers.

From *Long Walk to Freedom* by Nelson Mandela

[5]kraal – *hut*
[6]Xhosa – *a South African tribe*

Interpreting the meanings

1 Close read the two paragraphs starting '*From an early age ..*' to '*... one got the hang of it.*' Find evidence to show how Mandela's childhood was both similar to and different from your own. Present your information in a table like the one below:

Similarities	Differences
• Boys playing and fighting	• Shared food and blankets with the same boys
•	•
•	•

2 How do we know from this text that Mandela is proud of his upbringing and his homeland? Find four examples that demonstrate this pride, and **deduce** what is suggested by each one of your quotations. The first one is done for you.

He writes in the third paragraph: '*I learned to stick-fight – essential knowledge to any rural African boy – and became adept at its various techniques.*' This suggests that he is proud of having learned a necessary skill.

▶ Compare

Compare Text 3: A country childhood with one of the other texts. You are now going to explain the similarities and differences in attitudes towards young people in both texts.

1 You will need to scan the text to find the references or quotations you might need to help you to answer this question. Think about the way the texts deal with:

- things that happen to the young people
- young people's relationships with each other
- adults' attitudes towards young people
- young people's attitudes towards adults.

You should prepare your reading response in a table, like this:

Example from Text 3: A country childhood	Example from Text 1: The first week	How are they similar?	How are they different?
Mandela 'loses face' amongst his friends and feels humiliated	'Supposing no-one talks to me'	Both texts show the importance of the good opinion of your peer group	

2 Nelson Mandela writes about a childhood in rural Africa that had not changed for centuries. Compare it with your own upbringing. What are the advantages and disadvantages of the type of childhood Nelson Mandela describes? **Empathise.** Working with a partner, make some spider diagram notes and prepare a brief presentation for the rest of the class.

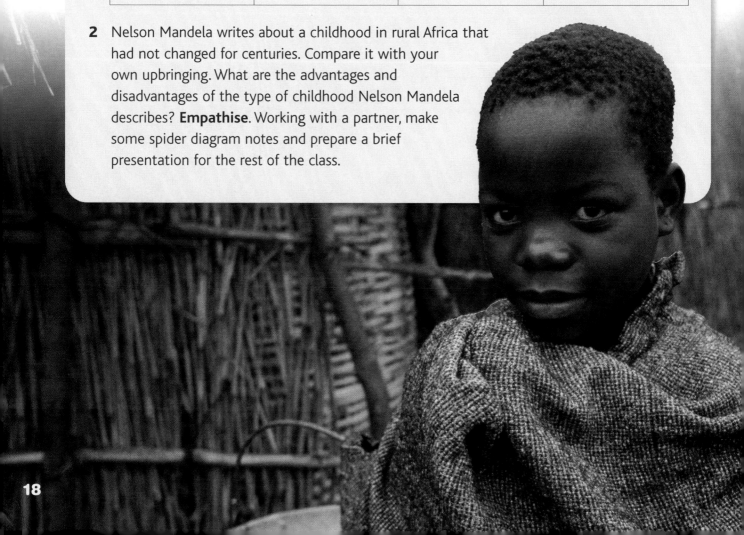

2 Emergencies

Introduction

Most of the time emergencies are something we see on television or read about in newspapers, and they seem to happen to other people, not to us. You are going to read three pieces of writing, all of which deal with very different sorts of emergencies. With any luck you won't ever face any situations quite like this – but if you do, you will now be prepared!

 Text 1 Air raid   **Text 2** Volcanoes   **Text 3** Snow shelters

Reading strategies

- relate to previous reading experience
- make judgements
- speculate
- infer
- see images
- ask questions
- feel
- re-read

Pre-reading: relate to previous reading experience

You are going to read three texts on the theme of emergencies:

- a piece of descriptive writing from a novel for teenagers
- a survival guide giving information
- a set of instructions about how to build a survival shelter.

The writer of each text uses very different language and vocabulary to get their ideas across to the reader.

1 Work with a partner to read each of the extracts a–f below. For each extract, say which text you think it comes from and your reasons for thinking this. You may think that an extract could come from one or more of the texts – if so, give a reason explaining why.

Extracts

a do not argue with the authorities

b gather several sticks about 60cm (2ft) long

c blue points of light hung motionless in the sky, brighter than the stars

d if you are travelling by car, be sure you have enough petrol

e dig a trench and make a roof by weaving branches together

f they were safe, because bombs always dropped in a curve in front of bombers.

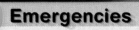
Emergencies

The novel *The Machine Gunners*, by Robert Westall, describes life in the Second World War from the point of view of a group of teenagers, who find themselves fighting their own war against the Nazis. In this text, the gang, led by Chas McGill, have just found a machine gun and are about to take it home, when they are caught in a violent air raid.

Air raid

Chas despaired. And then suddenly the night turned white, black, white, black, white. A great hammer banged on the dark tin tray of the sky, crushing their ear-drums again and again. Anti-aircraft guns.
Then, in the following silence, came the noise of an aircraft engine.

Chug-chug-chug-chug

'One of theirs,' whispered Cem. The dog whined and fled. Fatty Hardy shouted, and the whole group of bystanders were streaking away to the nearest shelter. Then that hammer was beating the sky again. Echoes of its blows rippled away, like someone slamming doors further and further off down a corridor.

Chas stared at the sky, trying to guess where the next white flashes would come from. They came in, in a scattered pattern moving west. Five at a time. That was the guns at the Castle. Then a group of three together. That was the guns at Willington Quay.

'What shall we do?' whispered Audrey.

'Take your bike and get to a shelter. We can manage without you.'

'But I shouldn't be out in the open during an air-raid.'

'You don't think these trees will shelter you from anything?' said Chas brutally. She went, wobbling wildly across the waste ground.

'What about us?' said Cem.

'I'm getting this gun home while the streets are empty. This air-raid's the best chance we got.'

'The wardens will stop us.'

'Not if we go by Bogie Lane.' Bogie Lane was a little-used cinder track that led through the allotments to near home. 'No one'll think of looking there.'

'Right, come on then.'

The blackness of night was back. As they dragged and bounced through the dark, the warning note of the air-raid siren sounded.

'Dozy swine. Caught asleep as usual,' said Cem in disgust.

'It's a sneak raider. They glide in without engines.'

'And he's hit something.' Cem nodded to the west, where a rapidly growing yellow glare was lighting up the rooftops.

'Or else they got *him*. Must be Howdon way.'

'Only the one. All-clear will sound in a minute.'

But it didn't. They were halfway up Bogie Lane when they heard the *chug-chug-chug* of enemy engines again.

'More than one.'

'Six or seven.'

Ahead, the night lit up as if great blue floodlights had been switched on. Blue points of light hung motionless in the sky, brighter than stars.

'They're dropping parachute flares.'

The *chug-chug-chug* grew nearer. They felt like two small flies crawling across a white tablecloth. Up there, thought Chas, Nazi bomb-aimers were staring down through black goggles, teeth clenched, hands tight on bomb-release toggles, waiting for the cross-hairs of their bomb-sights to meet on Bogie Lane and the two flies who crawled there.

Chug-chug-chug. Overhead now. They were safe, because bombs always dropped in a curve in front of bombers. He had watched them fall in newsreels of the Polish Campaign, out of black Stukas ...

Bang, bang, bang. The hammer was at it again, right overhead. This meant a new danger: falling shell-shrapnel. Chas could hear it, whispering and pattering down like steel rain all around.

'Go on!' screamed Chas. 'Get the bastards, kill the bastards!' Then silence, blackness, nothing. The parachute flares had gone out.

'Come on,' shouted Chas, dragging Cem to his feet. 'They'll be back in a minute.'

The bogie wheels crunched along the cinders, and they could hear the hard *knock, knock* of the machine-gun on the bogie's planks. They got back to the Square before trouble started again. A rough hand grabbed Chas's shoulder.

'Where the hell you been?' It was his father, wearing a tin hat. 'Your mother's worried sick.'

'She knew I was going down Chirton,' squawked Chas.

'Get down the shelter. Who's that with you?'

'Cem.'

'Get him down as well. I'll go and tell his mother he's safe.'

'What about the Guy?'

Mr McGill dragged the bogie roughly against the garden hedge. 'It'll have to take its chance.'

From *The Machine Gunners* by Robert Westall

Interpreting the meanings

1 Robert Westall makes it clear to the reader that Chas is the leader of the group. Read the text closely, noting down examples of Chas's leadership. **Make judgements** about how the following show that Chas is the leader:

- his relationship with Cem and Audrey
- the knowledge he has about the situation that they are in
- the ways in which he talks to the others.

Looking at language

2 Robert Westall describes the situation of being bombed so vividly that the reader can almost **see images** of what's happening and **feel** what the characters are feeling. He does this by using powerful descriptive language.

Find an example of each of the following techniques and explain its effect:

a onomatopoeia **b** simile **c** personification **d** metaphor.

Emergencies

Some emergencies can't easily be prepared for by anyone. Volcanic eruptions are one such problem. This text is intended to provide helpful information that may prove useful to people before, during and after a volcanic eruption.

Volcanoes

VOLCANOES

Volcanoes create the greatest natural explosions in the world.

They're spectacular, but deadly, and can change the shape of landscapes for ever.

If a volcano erupted at full strength you could expect some or all of the following:

- A continuous rain of smothering ash and super-heated mud
- Furnace-hot winds that flatten and burn everything in their path
- Fountains and rivers of molten lava
- Clouds of choking, suffocating gases
- Fiery rock bombs the size of cars
- Dense clouds that can obscure the sun for weeks
- Huge tidal waves (also known as tsunami) that can flatten coastal cities
- Staggering, ear-splitting noise

Volcanoes destroy.

WARNINGS

In recent years, satellites have been widely used to help detect imminent and increased volcanic activity around the world's hot spots. Satellite tracking systems can identify a build-up of the most common tell-tale gases and fluctuations in heat that may indicate an eruption is likely to occur.

Earth tremors or even earthquakes can also sometimes herald a major volcanic eruption.

If a volcano was about to blow near you, warnings would be issued from the local Disaster Prevention Office on the radio, in newspapers, on TV and by official monitors patrolling the surrounding affected areas.

You would be told:

- when the eruption is expected
- which area is most likely to be affected
- what type of eruption to expect
- the timetable for evacuation procedures

In some countries, warnings are also given by the ringing of church bells.

Despite improved warning systems, most volcanoes remain unpredictable. Even those considered dormant for many years can unexpectedly become active again.

continued

continued

EVACUATION!

If you lived close to an active volcano that was expected to erupt, you would have to be prepared to evacuate your home at short notice. You may have to travel on foot, by car or by truck or even by ship in coastal areas.

- **Do not** argue with the authorities if you are told to leave your home. It is for your own safety. In most places you would face a fine if you were to enter a forbidden zone near an active volcano.

- **Do** stay calm.

- **Do not** guess where you need to go. The experts can predict with some accuracy which areas are most likely to be affected.

- **Do** find out exactly where the safe havens are located. Emergency shelters are often set up in schools and community halls.

- **Do** leave everything behind that you don't need.

- **Do not** stay around to watch the spectacle. It may be an incredible sight, but the consequences are not worth the risk.

You could increase your chances of surviving a volcanic blast by wearing an Emergency Escape Hood, which was developed by the US Navy. The hood is placed over your head and a tube connected to a canister of compressed air allows you to breathe. However, even this would keep you alive for no more than thirty minutes.

Poisonous, evil-smelling sulphurous volcanic gas and odourless carbon dioxide are more lethal than lava, pumice or ash. The ejected gas can remove all oxygenated air from a very large area in a matter of minutes.

Lava 'ash flows' or 'glowing avalanches' can speed down a volcano at up to 100 kmph and would be impossible to outrun, which is why it is so important to evacuate the area as soon as possible.

THE JOURNEY

- If you are travelling by car, be sure you have enough petrol. Take a spare can of petrol. It may already be scarce and you will need all the supplies you can obtain.

- Dust off any ash or debris that may have accumulated on your car if it has been left out in the open.

- Check the engine. Electric cables can easily be torn or burned through by ash and pumice.

- Take plenty of bottled water or other drinks to quench your thirst throughout your journey. The heat and dry air near a volcano will make you especially thirsty.

- During the journey, you may need to keep on the wipers to clear any ash falling on the windscreen. Close all windows to avoid a build up of ash dust.

- Beware of ash bowls – large holes in the road filled to surface level with ash. They may be more than a metre deep, and like quicksand in places.

- If your vehicle is stuck, leave it and make your way on foot.

From *Survive Volcanic Fury* by Jack Dillon

Studying the structure

1   Begin by reading the text closely. It is divided into four sections: Volcanoes; Warnings; Evacuation and The Journey. In order to make it easier for someone to use the leaflet in an emergency situation, it would be helpful to break down each section into smaller parts, with subheadings that show clearly what each part is about.

Re-read the text to identify the important points in each section. Using the table below, suggest three subheadings for each of these smaller sections of text.

Section	Subheading 1	Subheading 2	Subheading 3
Volcanoes			
Warnings			
Evacuation			
The Journey			

2   You now have to create a warning poster for people living near to a volcano. You are allowed only 100 words of text to tell them what to do during a volcanic eruption. You may also use pictures and diagrams, but remember that a poster needs to be eye catching and to be able to be read quickly.

3   In a real emergency, how useful would this leaflet be to you? In what ways could it be made more helpful?

In exceptionally cold weather people have made good use of snow shelters to enable them to survive when caught in blizzard conditions. The text you are about to read gives a detailed explanation of how to build a snow shelter – it's information to read before you need to build one, not when you are actually caught in a snowstorm!

SNOW SHELTERS

Provided temperatures remain below 0°C (32°F), constructing snow shelters is relatively easy. Sheltering from the wind is the first priority, since the wind can drastically decrease the air temperature. Temperatures below −10°C (14°F) become increasingly unpleasant, so that it becomes necessary to construct shelters in which heat can be retained extremely well. These can range from a simple, hollowed-out heap of snow to an igloo, which can take a few hours to construct. In a long-term shelter, such as an igloo, heavy, cold air can be diverted away from the occupants by digging a cold sink to channel the air down and away from the shelter. It is important to allow for adequate ventilation in all snow shelters in order to prevent suffocation.

BUILDING AN IGLOO

1 Cut blocks from dry, hard snow, using a snow saw or large knife. Each block should be about 1 m (3 ft) long, 40 cm (15 in) high, and 20 cm (8 in) deep.

2 Form a circle with blocks around the hole created where you cut the blocks. Cut the circle in a spiral from the top of the last block to the ground ahead of the first block. This will make it easy to construct a dome.

3 Build up the walls, overlapping the blocks and shaping them so that they lean inwards. Cut a hole under the wall for the cold sink and entrance. Put several blocks along one wall as a sleeping platform.

WARNING

It is vital to make at least one airhole in the roof to avoid suffocation. The igloo will get very warm inside with heat from your body, even if it is cold and windy outside. Without ventilation, lethal carbon monoxide will build up.

BUILDING AN IGLOO

 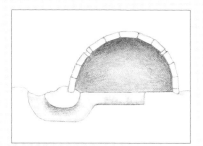 

4 The last block must initially be larger than the hole. Place the block on top of the igloo, then, from inside, shape and wiggle it to slot exactly into the hole.

5 Hot air from your body and stove rises, and is trapped inside the dome. Cold air falls into the sink and flows away to the outside. It is essential to cut ventilation holes in the walls with an ice axe.

Finished Igloo *With warmth inside the igloo, the surface of the walls will melt and freeze over, to form a smooth, airtight ice surface. Roof over entrance tunnel prevents snow from blowing into igloo.*

BUILDING A QUINZE

1 Place rucksacks and other equipment in a tight cone. The equipment will form the inside core of the shelter, and will reduce the amount of snow needed to build the quinze (pronounced "kwinzee").

2 Using a snowshoe or a spade, pile snow over the rucksacks, compacting it. Wait at least 30 minutes for the snow to freeze before adding more snow to build up the thickness of the dome.

3 When the snow in the pile is about 1 m (3 ft) thick, smooth the dome and leave it for about an hour to harden. This period is important, since it allows the snow to recrystallize, bonding the particles together.

4 Gather several sticks about 60 cm (2 ft) long. Push them into the snow all over the dome as depth guides, pointing to the centre of the quinze.

5 Dig down beside the quinze and burrow under the wall until you can carefully remove the rucksacks. Then excavate inside with a cooking pot until the ends of the sticks appear.

From *Outdoor Survival Guide* by Hugh McManners

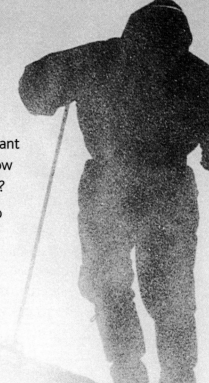

Explaining the ideas

1 Scan the text to find out the following:

    a How many different types of snow shelter are being described here, and what are their names?

    b **Make a judgement** about what the most important piece of information given about survival in a snow shelter is. Is this information repeated in the text?

    c Make an equipment list that would enable you to build both of the snow shelters described here.

2 Read the text closely. **Infer** to decide which of the statements in the list below are:

- literally true (the writer actually states them)

- inferentially true (the writer doesn't state them but the reader can work out from the text that they are true)

- incorrect (there is no evidence to back up the statements from the text).

Be prepared to give reasons for your answers.

    a Making snow shelters is easy providing the temperature is above 32°C.

    b You need to be reasonably fit and well to construct an igloo.

    c Warmth inside the igloo makes the walls melt and spoils the shelter.

    d You need to make a sleeping platform inside an igloo as you build it.

    e Humans find it difficult to survive in temperatures below 10°C.

    f As you build a quinze you will need to leave snow time to freeze.

Compare

1 Each of the texts you have studied about emergencies is very different. Refresh your memory of each text by copying out and completing the table below:

	Purpose of the text	Audience for whom text it is written	Why you think this
Text 1: Air raid			
Text 2: Volcanoes			
Text 3: Snow shelters			

2 Although each text is very different, they all give the reader a very clear impression of what the emergencies that they describe would be like. Skim read the three texts to help you to complete the table below.

	Main dangers to life	Key ways of avoiding death or injury	Most frightening aspects of the emergency
Text 1: Air raid			
Text 2: Volcanoes			
Text 3: Snow shelters			

3 Now choose one of the three texts to write your own imaginative account of the experience the writer describes, as if it had happened to you. **Empathise** and use as many details as possible from the information the text has given you. When you have completed the writing, which should be about 250–300 words, underline all the information that you have taken from the texts you have read.

You may wish to use one of the following sentences to start off your writing:

• Last night was the worst air raid of the war so far ...

• As soon as we heard the news broadcast we knew we had to get out. The volcano was ...

• The falling snow was getting thicker and faster, I began to think of ...

3 Healthy eating?

Introduction

As human beings, we all need to eat food to live but for some of us eating can become an obsession, whether this is about healthy eating or over indulging in our favourite fast food. We are bombarded with advice in newspapers, magazines and in advertising on what to eat, what not to eat and when to eat. The question is: 'How healthy is your diet?'

 Text 1 Junk food addicts may sue

 Text 2 Diet 2000

 Text 3 Ice cream fat stuns scientists

Reading strategies

- ask questions
- interpret patterns
- relate to previous reading experience
- reinterpret

Pre-reading: relate to previous reading experience

1 In pairs, think about two different advertisements for food you have read or seen recently (eg in a magazine, on TV or on a billboard). Discuss with your partner what kind of image of eating the advertisements portray and make bullet point notes of your comments. You may wish to consider the following points:

- the layout – what does it look like?
- the wording – is it easy to remember?
- the visuals/images – what can you see?
- the audience/who it is aimed at – who do they expect to buy and eat this product?

2 Compare notes with another pair in your group. Do you think advertisers promote healthy eating?

This text is taken from the *Daily Mail* newspaper. In this article, the writer, James Chapman, discusses the idea that eating certain kinds of foods may be as harmful to us as smoking cigarettes.

Junk food addicts may sue

by James Chapman

Junk food could be as addictive as cigarettes or heroin, according to explosive research which could pave the way for massive lawsuits against manufacturers.

The findings suggest that snacks high in fat or sugar can cause changes in the brain similar to those seen in people hooked on smoking or drugs.

It could open the floodgates for multi-million-pound actions against food firms by customers who say their health has been ruined by an 'addiction' to their products.

Similar steps taken by smokers have left the tobacco industry reeling, with thousands of Florida smokers winning £100billion in a class action[1] against manufacturers in 2000.

So far, the fast-food industry has fought off legal claims by arguing that individuals make a choice about what to eat and it is common knowledge that meals such as burgers and chips are fattening.

But proof that high-fat and high-sugar foods are addictive would dramatically strengthen the case for legal action. The question would then arise as to whether manufacturers knew their products to be addictive and continued to produce them regardless.

More than 300million people worldwide are clinically obese and therefore at risk of heart disease, diabetes, high blood pressure and osteoarthritis.

Around one in five British adults – 17 per cent of men and 21 per cent of women – is obese, triple the rate of 20 years ago.

In the last decade, the percentage of overweight children has virtually doubled. Several scientific teams around the world have produced evidence suggesting that the obesity epidemic may be due to the addictive nature of fatty and sugary foods.

Psychologists at Princeton University in New Jersey have shown that rats fed a diet containing 25 per cent sugar were thrown into a state of confusion and anxiety when the sugar was removed.

Their symptoms, including chattering

[1] class action – *a law-suit*

continued

continued

teeth and the shakes, were similar to those seen in humans suffering withdrawal from nicotine or morphine.

Scientists at Rockefeller University in New York found that regularly eating such products could reconfigure[2] the body's hormonal system to want yet more fat.

As people put on weight, they become more resistant to the hormone leptin, which is strongly linked to weight and appetite.

Leptin is secreted by fat cells and sends a signal to the brain when enough has been eaten. In overweight people, this signal does not work properly.

Research suggests that fatty meals may also make people over-produce a substance in the brain called galanin that stimulates eating.

Dr Sarah Leibowitz, of Rockefeller University, found that a single high-fat meal stimulates galanin production.

In another study, to be published shortly, Professor Ann Kelley, a neuroscientist, and Matthew Will, of the University of Wisconsin, found that fat rats underwent changes in brain development.

"The research suggests that a high-fat diet alters brain biochemistry with effects similar to those of powerful drugs, such as morphine," said Mr Will.

Research by experts at the University of Sussex, which is to be presented at a scientific meeting this week, suggests that high-fat foods stimulate 'pleasure chemicals' in the brain.

John Banzhaf, professor of law at the George Washington University law school, said companies selling food high in fat and sugar were 'deeply vulnerable' to legal action.

From the *Daily Mail* 14 July 2003

[2]**reconfigure** – *change*

Studying the structure

1 Scan the text and pick out six features that make it clear that this is a non-fiction text. **Relate to your previous reading experience.** You could look at the layout, the heading, the language and other features.

Explaining the ideas

2 **a** Skim read the text from the beginning to *'The question would then arise as to whether manufacturers knew their products to be addictive and continued to produce them regardless.'*

b Briefly explain why junk food might be as addictive as smoking cigarettes. What defence does the fast-food industry claim in response?

c Close read the section from *'More than 300 million people ...'* to *'... high-fat foods stimulate 'pleasure chemicals' in the brain.'* Pick out the key points from the research which show how fatty or sugary foods may be addictive or harmful.

d **Reinterpret** your findings with a partner. Do you think people should be able to sue fast-food companies if they become fat through eating their food? Have your ideas been changed by the text?

Healthy eating?

This text is taken from *Diet 2000*, an advice book given away with the magazine *New Woman*. In this extract the writer examines different kinds of foods and meals and gives advice on healthy eating.

Diet 2000

1 Breakfast

Breakfast really is an essential meal. Skipping the first meal of the day is one of the worst mistakes you can make and this applies as much to slimmers as to those who are happy with their weight. If you miss out on breakfast you may not have eaten for 15 or 16 hours and you will be lacking in energy by midday. Concentration goes and headaches and irritability take over. Start breakfast with a glass of freshly squeezed orange juice. Then choose from a bowl of cereals: Swiss muesli with milk and fresh fruit; porridge or cooked oatbran; toast (wholemeal) thinly spread with butter; homemade muffins; French bread and apricot jam; Swedish baked rolls or crispbread. Add fresh fruit, skimmed milk or low-fat yogurt and you'll have a really healthy start to the day.

Hidden hazards

Check the labels on your breakfast cereals as they vary greatly in their sugar, salt and fibre content. High sugar and salt aren't necessarily a problem but it's useful to know what you are adding to the day's total.

Salt
- **High content:**
  Shredded Wheat, Weetabix
- **Fairly high content:**
  Puffed Wheat

Sugar
- **High content:**
  Frosties, Crunchy Nut Cornflakes, Ricicles, Coco Pops, Sugar Puffs
- **Fairly high content:**
  All-Bran, Bran Buds, Bran Flakes, Sultana Bran, Oat Bran Flakes

Fibre
- **High content:**
  All-Bran, Bran Buds
- **Fairly high content:**
  Weetabix, Shredded Wheat, Bran Flakes, Sultana Bran

2 Main meals

The timing of your main meal, if you have one, will depend on your lifestyle and the demands of your job, leisure activities and family.

You can use your main meal to fill in any nutritional gaps from the rest of the day. Make sure you have some protein-rich food if you've been eating salads and fruit all day. Alternatively, add extra starchy food with plenty of fruit and vegetables if you've been subsisting on fatty snacks and junk food.

continued ▶

Here are some good menus for everyday healthy eating:

- Tomato soup with crusty rolls
- Ham and sweetcorn lasagne with green salad dressed with lemon juice
- Fruit kebabs

- Avocado with grapefruit
- Sesame chicken with stir-fry vegetables and rice
- Apricot yogurt

- Liver paté with toast
- Gujarati cabbage with rice and grilled tomatoes
- Fresh fruit

- Minestrone soup
- Jacket potatoes stuffed with mushrooms and bacon, green salad
- Peaches and ice-cream

- Bean and tuna salad
- Wholemeal pasta with pesto sauce
- Watercress and carrot salad with apples

3 Snacks and light meals

As life gets more hectic, you tend to eat snacks more often. There's nothing wrong with this. Provided you choose the right kind of food, a snack meal can be as healthy as any other. Healthy snacks are sometimes seen as time-consuming to make but a wholesome granary bread sandwich filled with tuna and salad takes no longer to make than a rather less healthy one filled with roast beef, lettuce and mayonnaise.

When making sandwiches, slice the bread fairly thickly (it doesn't have to be doorsteps) and either omit the butter or margarine altogether or spread very thinly. Fill unbuttered pitta loaves or hollowed-out bread sticks for a change.

Ideas for fillings

- Liver paté or liver sausage and watercress.

- Mixed grated Cheddar cheese and grated raw carrots. Toss the carrot in a little oil to stop it discolouring and losing its goodness.

- Sliced bananas and dates, moistened with a little lemon juice.

- Sliced mangoes layered with cottage cheese and mint.

- Finely chopped chicken mixed with chopped tomatoes and basil.

- Drained and mashed sardines mixed with a little vinegar and black pepper and layered with beetroot.

From *Diet 2000*

Studying the structure and looking at language

1   Skim the three sections of the text and identify any features of the layout which the writer uses to emphasise certain points (eg bold type, bullet points, etc).

2   Scan the three sections and pick out imperative verbs (command words like 'add', 'choose' and 'start') which the writer uses to give advice to the reader.

3   Can you **identify any patterns** in the way that the layout features and imperative verbs have been used by the writer? Discuss your ideas with a partner.

Explaining the ideas

4   Close read all three sections of the extract. Ask yourself which you think are the most important two pieces of advice in each section and record these in a table.

Text 3 **Healthy eating?**

This text is an article from the broadsheet newspaper, *The Guardian*. In this article, the journalist discusses research which suggests that ice cream may be more unhealthy and fattening than we think.

Ice cream fat stuns scientists

David Adam, science correspondent

Ice creams and milkshakes bought from parlours that are springing up in shopping centres and cinemas across Britain can contain more fat and calories than burgers and pizzas, US researchers have found.

In some cases a single dessert contains two days' worth of saturated fat, while others are the calorific equivalent of an entire meal. The researchers admit, while they hardly expected to find ice cream a health food, they found the results staggering.

"It's as if these ice cream shops were competing to see who could inflict the greatest toll on our arteries and waistlines," said Jayne Hurley, a nutritionist with the Centre for Science in the Public Interest in Washington DC, which undertook the research.

Researchers found that a Ben and Jerry's waffle cone dipped in chocolate and filled with a single scoop of "chunky monkey" ice cream had more saturated fat than a pound of spare ribs, while a Haagen-Dazs sundae called the Mint Chip Dazzler was equal to eating a T-bone steak, caesar salad and a baked potato with sour cream on the side.

The centre said that calorie counts should be included on menus, so customers could see what they were eating.

A single scoop of ice cream provides 250 to 350 calories and half a day's worth of saturated fat. Add the cone and fudge, nuts and whipped cream, and the treats regularly tip the scales over the 1,000 calorie mark and include more than 30g of saturated fat – more than in three McDonald's quarter pounders.

Most of the numbers came from the producing companies themselves, but the researchers sent a dozen items from outlets across the US for which the chains did not supply data to an independent laboratory for analysis.

The laboratory also estimated sugar content, which the companies did not divulge.

The findings are published in the latest edition of the centre's newsletter.

Even seemingly healthier options like frozen yoghurt drinks are regularly dosed with fatty syrups and candy pieces.

"Frozen yoghurt is lower in fat than ice cream, but I doubt that people [expect] the calories and saturated fat of two pork chops, a caesar salad and a buttered baked potato – just in a drink," Ms Hurley said.

From The Guardian

Looking at language and how the reader feels

1 According to this article, ice cream is not as healthy as we might think. Skim read the article and identify the main findings of the researchers.

2 Scan the text and pick out any words or phrases which suggest why this article was written by the science correspondent. **Relate to your previous reading experience** to help you answer this question.

3 The researchers found their own results very surprising. For example in paragraph two of the article it states *'A single dessert contains two days' worth of saturated fat while others are the calorific equivalent of an entire meal.'* Close read the rest of the article and find two more comparisons between ice cream and other foods. **Ask questions**. What effect do you think these comparisons have on the reader? Why do you think the writer has used them?

Compare

You are now going to compare the different information given in these three texts about healthy and unhealthy food or eating by answering the following questions.

1 Both Text 1 and Text 3 use research as evidence to support their argument. Both of these texts are taken from newspapers.

   a Which text do you find most convincing?

   b How do the writers present the evidence of the researchers to make it more interesting?

2 In Text 2: Diet 2000 the writer organises the advice in a particular way.

   a How does the structure and layout help to make the case for healthy eating?

   b Compare the other two texts with Text 2. How far does their layout and structure differ?

3 Collate all the information you have gathered from these three texts. You are going to use this to write a leaflet for your school canteen promoting healthy eating. Before you begin to design and write your leaflet, discuss your findings in a group and decide how you will present your information. You will need to consider the following:

   • what information you want to get across
   • the audience – who will read the leaflet
   • the language – the words you will use to promote healthy eating
   • the design and layout – how best to arrange the information.

Your leaflet should be no more than 300 words.

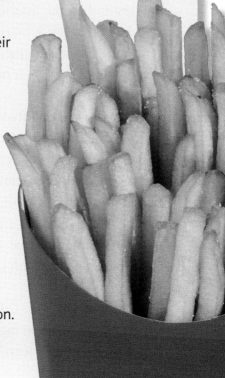

Saving animals

Introduction

We share our planet with many different animals but we don't always treat them well. Around the world, some animals are dying out. Others suffer because we don't help them. Some do not live free in the wild any more. For some people animal welfare is very important and they want to do everything they can to understand animals better and save them from pain or death. What are your views on the way people treat animals? Would you help an animal in distress?

 Text 1 How much do you care about wildlife?

 Text 2 Turtle rescue

 Text 3 Zoos – the arguments

Reading strategies

- see images
- hear a reading voice
- feel
- re-read

Pre-reading: see images

1 When we read, we often picture the ideas in our heads. We can add images to the words from our imagination or experiences. **Re-read** the introduction to this unit. As you read, think about the pictures that you can see in your head. These are the ideas that you bring to the reading of the text. Are they still pictures or moving images?

2 Share your images with a partner. Did you see the same things or different things?

3 Together, imagine the introduction is going to be a trailer advertising a TV programme called 'Saving Animals'. The purpose of a trailer is to persuade viewers to tune in to the programme. Your decisions about images will give them a visual clue of what they can expect to see. Either describe which images to include or draw a storyboard of the TV trailer. A storyboard is a sequence of rough sketches showing each scene. It helps the director see what the film will look like before filming starts.

Saving animals

The WWF (formerly known as The World Wildlife Fund) is the global environment network that protects wild animals and the places they live. It relies on donations from the public to support its work. This letter is not simply the usual request for money. Instead, it asks for people's views on the issues that concern the charity. The answers will help them to campaign more effectively. Of course, it also gives readers a chance to give!

WWF-UK Panda House, Weyside Park, Catteshall Lane, Godalming, Surrey GU7 1XR

WILDLIFE SURVEY 2003

How much do you care about wildlife?

Dear Householder,

We know that Britain is an animal-loving nation. And we know that many people are aware of the threat to many species of animals in the wild. What we don't quite know is how strongly people feel about the threat – whether, for instance, they believe that conservation of the British countryside is more important than tackling depletion of the ozone layer. Or whether it's justifiable to use tiger bones, for example, in Chinese medicine. Your area has been selected as one in which we are trying to establish the reactions of ordinary British people to the issues of wildlife, the extinction of species and environmental matters in general.

How important is it to save him?

Many of your neighbours will be receiving this same questionnaire and I do hope you can find the time to complete it, for the answers you give us will be invaluable as we plan future campaigns to protect wildlife.

WWF's position is quite clear. We are committed to help protect all species on Earth – mammals, fish, birds, plants and insects. That's why we are so alarmed at the rate at which many species are disappearing.

And that is why we are campaigning on behalf of the world's threatened species and habitats. But, hand in hand with that campaign to raise money for our work, we have decided to solicit your opinions on the subject.

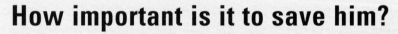

Does it matter if they become extinct?

Naturally, and because we are a charity, we are giving you the chance to become a supporter of WWF for as little as £2 a month. But do let me make it quite clear that we want your answers to this survey whether or not you decide to support WWF.

Hundreds of thousands will be involved in the research exercise. It will take you just a few minutes to answer these simple questions and the reply envelope enclosed will cost you nothing to send back.

Let me thank you in advance for your co-operation.

Your contribution counts. Call 08705 66 88 99 to set up a Direct Debit and join WWF

WILDLIFE SURVEY 2003

CONFIDENTIAL

Please try to answer all the questions, then fill in your name and address and send it back to WWF in the envelope enclosed.

1   **Do you think it matters if a species becomes extinct?**

Yes, a lot ☐   Yes, a little ☐

Not really ☐

2   **Tiger bones and rhino horn are used in traditional oriental medicine and the species are facing extinction as a result. Do you think their use is justified?**

Yes ☐

Yes, because people are
entitled to their own cultural beliefs ☐

Not at all ☐

3   **Have you ever seen any of these in the British Isles?**

Otter ☐   Badger ☐

Kingfisher ☐   Red Squirrel ☐

Pine Marten ☐

4   **WWF's work is concerned with a wide number of areas. What do you think are the priorities? (please rate very important, important or not very important)**

Threatened species

VERY IMP ☐   IMP ☐   NOT IMP ☐

Pollution and consumption

VERY IMP ☐   IMP ☐   NOT IMP ☐

Conservation of the British countryside

VERY IMP ☐   IMP ☐   NOT IMP ☐

Oceans and marine life

VERY IMP ☐   IMP ☐   NOT IMP ☐

Forests

VERY IMP ☐   IMP ☐   NOT IMP ☐

Depletion of the ozone layer and climate change

VERY IMP ☐   IMP ☐   NOT IMP ☐

Environmental education

VERY IMP ☐   IMP ☐   NOT IMP ☐

continued ▶

continued

5 Do you buy the following items?

Peat free garden grow bags ☐

Recycled paper products ☐

Organically grown fruit or vegetables ☐

Energy efficient appliances ☐

Unleaded petrol ☐

6 Do you try to recycle these items?

Paper ☐   Cans ☐

Bottles and glass ☐   Plastic ☐

7 Is your age:

Under 18 ☐   36-50 ☐

18-25 ☐   51-70 ☐

26-35 ☐   Over 70 ☐

8 And, are you?

Male ☐

Female ☐

9 Would you like to receive information on any of the following WWF products?

WWF credit card (123) ☐

WWF Guide to Making a Will (104) ☐

Fundraising Events (110) ☐

WWF Adoptions (541) ☐

From WWF

Explaining the ideas

1 Quickly skim read the whole text. Take no more than 20 seconds.
   Which bits of the text caught your attention? Make a list of these.

2 **a** Now close read the text. Check that you know how to say all of the words. Work out what any new words mean. You could look at the meaning of the whole sentence, using your knowledge of similar words or a dictionary.

   b **Re-read** the text, thinking about the **reading voice you can hear.** In a small group, prepare a reading of the text. Take a section each and make it sound really persuasive.

3 Look again at the first paragraph of the text and the survey.

   a Create a table like the one below. List the issues from paragraph 1 on which the writer wants to know our views. The first one has been written for you.

   b Then match the questions from the survey to this list. There might be more than one question for each issue.

Things they want to know our views on	Question number in the survey
How strongly people feel about the threat to animals in the wild.	1

Saving animals

> This is an extract from a novel, written in the form of a diary. In the novel, 14-year-old Laura tells of her life on the Isles of Scilly (near Cornwall) at the beginning of the twentieth century. Here, she writes about how she tried to save a giant turtle that was stranded on the beach.

TURTLE RESCUE

September 8th

He was upside down on the sand. I pulled the seaweed off him. His eyes were open, unblinking. He was more dead than alive, I thought. His flippers were quite still, and held out to the clouds above as if he was worshipping them. He was massive, as long as this bed, and wider. He had a face like a two hundred year old man, wizened and wrinkled and wise with a gently-smiling mouth.

I dug a deep hole in the sand beside him. I would lever him up and topple him in. I drove the spar into the sand underneath his shell. I drove it in again and again, until it was as deep as I could get it. I hauled back on it and felt him shift. I threw all my weight on it and at last he tumbled over into the hole, and the right way up, too. But when I scrambled over to him, his head lay limp in the sand, his eyes closed to the world. There wasn't a flicker of life about him. He was dead. I was quite sure of it now. It's silly, I know – I had only known him for a few minutes – but I felt I had lost a friend.

When Laura returns to the beach the next day, she discovers that the turtle is still alive but very weak and still cannot make it to the safety of the water.

September 9th

I told him what he had to do.

'You've got to walk the rest,' I said. 'You want to get back in the sea, you've got to walk, you hear me?'

He tried. He honestly tried. Time and again he dug the edge of his flippers into the sand, but he just couldn't move himself.

The flippers dug in again, again, but he stayed where he was. I tried pushing him from behind. That didn't work. I tried moving his flippers for him one by one. That didn't work. I slapped his shell. I shouted at him. All he did was swallow and blink at me. In the end I tried threatening him. I crouched down in front of him.

continued

41

continued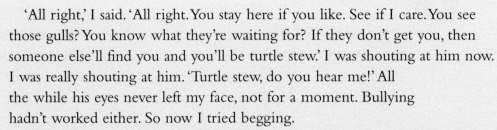

'All right,' I said. 'All right. You stay here if you like. See if I care. You see those gulls? You know what they're waiting for? If they don't get you, then someone else'll find you and you'll be turtle stew.' I was shouting at him now. I was really shouting at him. 'Turtle stew, do you hear me!' All the while his eyes never left my face, not for a moment. Bullying hadn't worked either. So now I tried begging.

'Please,' I said, 'please.' But his eyes gave me the answer I already knew. He could not move. He hadn't the strength. There was nothing else left to try. From the look in his eyes I think he knew it too.

I looked down at him. He was nudging at the sand with his chin, his mouth opening. He was hungry! I don't know why I hadn't thought of it before. I had no idea at all what turtles eat. So I tried what was nearest first – seaweed of all sorts, sea lettuce, bladderwrack, whatever I could find.

I dangled it in front of his mouth, brushing his nose with it so he could smell it. He looked as if he was going to eat it. He opened his mouth slowly and snapped at it. But then he turned his head away and let it fall to the ground. 'What then?' I asked.

A sudden shadow fell across me. Granny May was standing above me in her hat.

'How long have you been there?' I asked.

'Long enough,' she said and she walked around me to get a better look at the turtle.'

She told me to dig out a bowl in the sand, right under the turtle's chin, and then she shook out her net. He looked mildly interested for a moment and then looked away. It was no good. Granny May was looking out to sea, shielding her eyes against the glare of the sun.

'I wonder,' she murmured. 'I wonder. I shan't be long.' And she was gone, down to the sea. She was wading out up to her ankles, then up to her knees, her shrimping net scooping through the water around her. I stayed behind with the turtle and threw more stones at the gulls. When she came back, her net was bulging with jellyfish, blue jellyfish. She emptied them into the turtle's sandy bowl. At once he was at them like a vulture, snapping, crunching, swallowing, until there wasn't a tentacle left.

'Feel better now?' I asked, and I wondered if turtles burp when they've eaten too fast. He didn't burp, but he did move. The flippers dug deeper. He shifted – just a little at first. And then he was scooping himself slowly forward, inching his way through the sand. I went loony. I was cavorting up and down like a wild thing, and Granny May was just the same. The two of us whistled and whooped to keep him moving, but we knew soon enough that we didn't need to. Every step he took was stronger, his neck reaching forward purposefully. Nothing would stop him now. As he neared the sea, the sand was tide-ribbed and wet, and he moved ever faster, faster, past the rock pools and across the muddy sand where the lug-worms leave their curly casts. His flippers were under the water now. He was half walking, half swimming. Then he dipped his snout into the sea and let the water run over his head and down his neck. He was going, and suddenly I didn't want him to. I was alongside him, bending over him.

'You don't have to go,' I said.

'He wants to,' said Granny May. 'He has to.'

He was in deeper water now, and with a few powerful strokes he was gone, cruising out through the turquoise water of the shallows to the deep blue beyond. The last I saw of him he was a dark shadow under the sea making out towards Samson.

I felt suddenly alone.

From *The Wreck of the Zanzibar* by Michael Morpurgo

Explaining the ideas

1 a Use continuous reading to enjoy the story told in these extracts and become familiar with the content. As you read, try to create **images** in your head from what the words suggest to you.

b In pairs, choose a short section that you enjoyed and **re-read** it. Discuss and draw the images you pictured in your head and try to build up a more detailed picture. Label the picture with details from the text.

How the reader feels

2 What feelings does the writer want you to have about the characters and events?

a **Re-read** the entry for September 8th and note down your feelings about the events described.

b Now **re-read** the following three sections from the diary entry for September 9th. Note down your **feelings** during each section and try to explain why you felt that way.

- From *'I told him what he had to do'* to *'I think he knew it too.'*
- From *'I looked down at him'* to *'... let it fall to the ground.'*
- From *'A sudden shadow fell across me'* to the end of the text.

Text 3 Saving animals

This text presents two letters about zoos. Each letter presents a different set of arguments and tries to persuade you to agree. The first supports the view that zoos are like prisons while the second argues that zoos do have a valuable role to play. Together, they are analysing the issue and commenting from different viewpoints.

Zoos – the arguments

Zoo Check, Cherry Tree Cottage, Coldharbour, Dorking, Surrey RHS 6HA

Most young people have been to the zoo, taken there either by their parents or by their teacher. Perhaps you are one of them? If you are, your visit was probably described as a 'treat', a 'good day out', or a 'surprise'. But I wonder what you really felt as you wandered round from cage to cage?

If you like nature and wildlife I am sure you watch the wonderful films we have on television nowadays, films that show you animals living in their natural environment. I am always amazed that, through television, I am now able to eavesdrop on the lives of animals like the polar bear, the gorilla and the tiger – species from all round the world.

How does wildlife on television compare with the wildlife in the zoo? In the zoo do you see the polar bear hunting the vast icy wastes of the Arctic for seals, or digging a 'snow cave' in which to raise its cubs? Do you watch the mother teaching her young how to survive in that harsh and difficult climate? Or do you see the massive male silverback gorilla quietly leading his family through the African jungle, showing them which plants are good to eat, a watchful eye alert for any danger? Does the tiger in the zoo use its incredible camouflage to stalk its prey and then with a burst of speed race in for the kill?

What do you see and what do you learn at the zoo?

All over the world wildlife needs our help. Zoos say that they are vital centres for conserving animals that are threatened with extinction. But though in the past 150 years zoos have 'saved' perhaps twenty species, we are now losing one species every day! So does the answer to the conservation crisis lie with the zoos? Or is the answer that we – each of us – makes a pledge to help save the wild areas of the world and the huge variety of wildlife they contain without resorting to the unnatural captivity of the zoo? The choice is ours.

Next time you go to the zoo, ask yourself three questions: Why am I here? Why are the animals here? And are zoos any more than outdated prisons?

Perhaps we will never know, but I always wonder what the polar bear is thinking as it walks a few paces this way, a few paces that, its horizon a blue-rinsed concrete wall, its ocean a small paddling pool, and its future an unfulfilled life of boredom in captivity.

London Zoo
Regent's Park
London NW1 4RY

Some people imagine that the only place animals should be seen is in the wild and that to keep them in zoos is cruel. This is not true. Like us, all animals have basic needs for food, water, shelter and security. They need to be able to exercise, explore their environment, behave normally, and be with other animals of their own kind when they want to be. Good zoos make every effort to satisfy these requirements, while at the same time creating an environment where the animals are free from the stress of disease and predators.

Of course, not all zoos are the same. Keeping animals in bad zoos is inexcusable, but good zoos, where the animals are well taken care of, have a very valuable contribution to make to science, conservation and education. Zoos such as London, New York, San Diego and Washington, for example, have large research programmes which not only investigate animal behaviour and physiology, but also provide information and skilled personnel for projects in the wild. Anaesthetic techniques developed for the Giant Panda at London Zoo, for example, make it possible to handle this rare animal safely in China. Zoos also support scientists in the field by paying their salaries or by providing them with training and technical expertise essential to the success of the project in the wild.

Zoos also contribute to the conservation of species. The Arabian oryx was extinct in nature, but thanks to a co-operative zoo breeding programme this beautiful antelope is now back in the wild in the deserts of Oman. Plans are now well under way for similar projects for other species of desert wildlife in Arabia and Africa.

The conservation of African rhinos, Kouprey (a species of wild cattle), Partula snails and Asian Arawana fish are all additional examples of major international projects to combine the best of zoo-developed technology with programmes to save the species in the wild. The resources available from the zoos are vital to these projects if they are to achieve their long-term aims.

It is sadly true that less and less of the 'wild' exists now for the animals to live in. Even where there is the space, it may be impossible to protect them from hunters, starvation or loss of suitable habitat. Zoos are not a replacement for nature, but they are a way of helping it to survive.

From *Whose side are you on?* by Michael Forrester

45

Explaining the ideas

1   In pairs, close read a different letter each. From each paragraph, identify one sentence that makes the main point. Share these with your partner to provide a summary of the argument.

2   Decide which letter the following statements are from and find a quotation to support each one.

    a   Zoos have helped to save many animals.

    b   You can see animals better on television.

    c   Zoo scientists learn a lot about looking after animals in zoos and in the wild.

    d   Animals can't have a proper life in a zoo.

    e   Zoos bring in money to fund projects in the wild.

    f   Zoos haven't saved many animals from becoming extinct.

2   Now close read the other argument that you didn't read before. As you read, think about the **images that you can see**. Share them with a partner and talk about why you think you have seen these particular pictures.

Looking at language

3   Choose the text that you agree with and explain how the writer has persuaded you to agree with that point of view. Think about:

*   the words the writer uses – eg to describe the animals and to express an opinion

*   the choice of examples – eg are they familiar animals or ones you don't know? How does this persuade you?

*   whether the writer speaks directly to you or not – eg does the writer ask you questions? Does the writer use 'you'? Why is this effective?

*   the types of sentences used – eg short sentences like *'The choice is ours'* or *'This is not true'*.

▶ Compare

The first text in this unit included a survey. Here is a survey for you to copy out and complete. It will help you to explain the ideas in the different texts you have read and think about your reactions to them.

1 a In each text, which fact concerned you the most about the dangers animals are in?

Text 1:
- tiger bones are used in Chinese medicine OR
- many species like rhinos are disappearing OR
- a different fact (please state).

Text 2:
- stranded turtles would be killed and eaten as a stew OR
- gulls would attack and eat the turtle OR
- a different fact (please state).

Text 3:
- we are losing one species every day OR
- animals in the wild suffer because of hunters and starvation OR
- a different fact (please state).

b Which text concerned you the most about the dangers animals are in? Give a reason.

2 a What **images did you see** when you read each text?
- Text 1:
- Text 2:
- Text 3:

b Which text helped you to **see images** the best? Give a reason.

3 a What **feelings did you have** when you read each text? For each, state whether you felt pleased, relieved, worried, upset or a different emotion (please state). You might have felt more than one emotion for each text.
- Text 1:
- Text 2:
- Text 3:

b Which text made you **feel** the strongest emotions? Give a reason.

4 a If you could give money to an animal charity, which would it be? Number the following from 1–4 indicating the order of your choice of charity:
- London Zoo
- Save the Turtles
- WWF
- Zoo Check

b Give a reason.

Thank you for completing this survey!

5 Sport

Introduction

We all have dreams and ambitions when we are young, whether it is to become a famous footballer or to climb Mount Everest. Sometimes, however, we face obstacles and challenges along the way and it takes courage and determination to succeed against the odds. The texts in this unit explore the ways sportspeople in different fields have succeeded in their ambitions. You might not have experienced the exact problems described in these texts, but as you read, keep in mind how you have felt at times when you have faced a challenge.

 Text 1 Swimming against the tide

 Text 2 Bend It Like Beckham

 Text 3 First dive

Reading strategies

- see images
- hear a reading voice
- ask questions
- make judgements
- interpret patterns
- deduce

Pre-reading: interpret patterns

1   Think about two people you have heard about (eg in a novel, magazine article, newspaper or television programme) who managed to achieve an ambition in spite of the obstacles or difficulties they faced. Make notes about each one, recording what the obstacles were and how they overcame them to succeed.

2   Compare notes with a partner and discuss the types of adversity facing the people you have chosen (eg illness or disability, prejudice, lack of sponsorship etc). List these under the heading 'Obstacles to success'. Can you **identify any patterns** in the types of difficulty faced?

3   As a class discuss the qualities that you think these people possessed which allowed them to triumph over adversity. Are there any common features which all of them possess? List them under the heading 'Overcoming adversity'. (Keep this list for use later in the unit.)

Sport

This text is a newspaper article from *The Guardian* about Tim Reddish, a talented swimmer who won a silver medal in the Paralympic Games. In this extract the writer describes how Tim lost his sight and how he eventually became an Olympic athlete.

Swimming against the tide

Tim Reddish, Paralympic medallist, defies every prejudice about disability. *Kendra Inman reports.*

Ploughing down the lanes of an Olympic swimming pool represents freedom for Tim Reddish, Paralympic silver medallist. "When I'm in the pool, I'm free. I've not got a guide dog or a white cane, I'm doing something that I enjoy and I'm good at. If you looked across the pool you wouldn't even know that I was blind." Reddish's triumph at the 1996 Atlanta Paralympics was the result of years of punishing training schedules of anything up to 20 hours a week in the run-up to a competition. Like all world-class athletes, he is driven to succeed – and doesn't believe his disability has held him back.

Reddish's swimming career began as a youngster in Nottingham, in the days before he lost his sight. In 1988, aged 31, he was diagnosed with a degenerative eye condition called retinitis pigmentosa.

An estimated 25,000 people in the UK have RP, the name given to a group of hereditary disorders that affect the retina. The condition usually causes vision to deteriorate slowly over the years. Some people lose all sight; others retain partial vision into old age. The discovery came out of the blue, says Reddish, who had assumed that his habit of bumping into things was due to run-of-the-mill short-sightedness.

"I thought that there was a strong possibility that it would get a little worse, and then stabilise."

However, as time went on his vision deteriorated; now he can perceive light, but no more.

About a year after the diagnosis his life took a new turn when a friend returned from competing in the Seoul Olympics and told him about the Paralympics, for people with disabilities. The competition captured his interest, and he began to take swimming seriously again.

continued

continued

Disabled athletes face their biggest problems when they are training, says Reddish. Getting to the gym or track or pool presents the first hurdle (his pool is 50 minutes away, via two buses). Once there, swimmers who can't see the clock need someone at the poolside to help them keep pace.

During competitions, coaches tap swimmers on the head with a white cane with a ball on the end to alert them to turn.

"You don't see your opponents or the next lanes, so you swim straight and race hard every time. When you are swimming heats before the finals you sometimes find you're there miles before everyone else is."

Blind swimmers trust the poolside coaches to prevent them crashing into the sides of the pool. But things don't always go to plan: Reddish has crashed badly and ended up tangled in lane ropes.

Out of the pool, his impairment has not prevented him from doing anything he wants to, he says. "Most things are possible with some kind of adaptation or with some sort of guidance."

"I don't regard myself as disabled," he continues. "I think of myself as having an impairment, not a handicap or a disability. I'm not in the disability movement. The disabled people I work and associate with are involved in sport. We have a common goal: we are sports people first and disabled people second."

Since his sight deteriorated, Reddish has encountered "a lack of awareness rather than outright discrimination". He says, "People assume that because you are blind you can't do something. I discuss it and get into a dialogue with them and get to the root of the problem that way. Sometimes I have to compromise, sometimes they do."

Reddish is a firm believer in equality and won't accept anything less. He is a self-confessed extrovert, and doesn't balk[1] at being bolshie[2] when the occasion demands. "I want to be treated the same as my able-bodied peers. My philosophy is that you have the right to be provided with the same opportunities as everyone else."

But he argues that people with disabilities have to earn that right by "getting on with it". This attitude, he says, has met with criticism from some members of the disability movement.

Although the silver medal was the pinnacle of his swimming career, he retired from competitive swimming soon after and switched to the triathlon. Disappointment at failing to secure the Paralympic gold medal, coupled with a feeling that he was getting too old, lay behind the decision. But the need to compete won out, and after being hauled out of retirement aged 41 to join a relay team last year, he won a string of medals.

He has now returned to serious competition and hankers after that elusive gold medal. The first chance at gold will be at the European championships this August, followed by the Paralympics in Sydney next year. Neither age nor disability is a barrier, he says. "When the swimmer who has come second is 17 years old, and I've just kicked his ass, I get a real buzz."

From *The Guardian*

---

[1]**balk** – *shy away from*   [2]**bolshie** – *outspoken*

Looking at language

1 Skim read the extract. Why do you think the writer uses this title 'Swimming against the tide'? Think about the following to help you **deduce**:

- the literal and metaphorical meaning of the title
- the context of the article and how it relates to the title
- the viewpoint of Tim Reddish.

Make notes on your findings and compare them with a partner.

Explaining the ideas

2 Close read the extract from *'Disabled athletes face their biggest problems when they are training, says Reddish'* to the paragraph which finishes *'Sometimes I have to compromise, sometimes they do.'* What are the main difficulties faced by disabled athletes as described in this extract?

3 Close read the rest of the article and summarise Tim Reddish's own view of his loss of sight and disability. In pairs discuss his views and your own on this topic.

Sport

This is an extract from a novel set in modern day England, about a young British Asian girl whose hero and role model is David Beckham. In this extract she dreams of becoming a footballer and playing for Manchester United and England but she faces tough opposition from her family, and her mother in particular.

Bend It Like Beckham

Old Trafford. Manchester United v. Anderlecht. The crowd a sea of red and white. They're on edge, waiting for the all-important goal.

'But there's a big question mark hanging over Manchester United,' John Motson says breathlessly. 'Where's the goal going to come from? Will it be Scholes? Could it be Ryan Giggs? Or will David Beckham himself break through?'

The crowd lean forward, urging the players on. The atmosphere is electric.

'Oh, and there's the ball Beckham wanted! Plenty of players in the middle, and Bhamra's making ground as well. It's a decent cross, and there's Bhamra. That's a fine header – AND SHE SCORES!'

The crowd go wild.

'And it's a goal by Jess Bhamra! A superb header, beating the defender and planting the ball just out of reach past the goalkeeper. Jess Bhamra makes a name for herself at Old Trafford! Have we discovered a new star here, Gary?'

Back in the TV studios, Gary Lineker turns to Alan Hansen and John Barnes. They all look well impressed.

'Good question, Motty,' says Gary, turning to the panel. '*Could* Jess Bhamra be the answer to England's prayers, Alan?'

Alan raises his eyebrows. 'There's no denying the talent there, Gary. She's quick-thinking, comfortable on the ball, she's got awareness and vision. I tell you what, I wish she was playing for Scotland.'

Gary laughs and turns to John Barnes. 'John, do you think England have found the player to help relive our 1966 World Cup glory?'

'No question, Gary,' says John. 'I think we've finally got the missing piece of the jigsaw. And, the best thing is, she's not even reached her peak yet.'

Gary turns to the camera. 'Now, joining us in the studio is Jess's mother, Mrs Bhamra.'

MUM?! Get out of my fantasy!

'So, Mrs Bhamra, you must be very proud of your daughter?' Gary beams.

'Not at all!' shrieks Mum. 'She shouldn't be running around with all these men, showing her bare legs to seventy thousand people. She's bringing shame on her family –' she gives the panel a filthy look '– and you three shouldn't be encouraging her.'

Gary, Alan and John look like little boys who've just been told off by their teacher.

'Jesminder, you get back home right now!' Mum rants on, pointing her finger at the camera. 'Wait till I get hold of you! Jesminder ...'

A second later, my bedroom door crashed open.

'Jesminder, are you listening to me?' Mum demanded.

Why did she always have to interrupt at the best bits? Gary was about to interview Sven-Goran Eriksson, who was considering calling me up for the next England match.

'Jesminder, have you gone mad?' Mum pointed at the TV and glared at me. Her special *Listen to me, I'm your mother and I know best* glare. 'Football shootball! It's your sister's engagement party tomorrow, and you're sitting here watching that skinhead boy.'

She grabbed the remote control from me, and snapped the TV off. I groaned.

'Oh, *Mum*, it's Beckham's corner.'

Mum took no notice. She never does. 'Come downstairs,' she ordered me. 'Your sister's going crazy.'

Tell me something I don't know. Pinky's pretty crazy, anyway. Now,

continued

continued

with her wedding coming up, she's a full-on lunatic. I could hear her downstairs right now, having a fit about something or other.

I stood up with a sigh. My bedroom was the only place I could really chill out, but even here I couldn't get any peace and quiet half the time. I had the room exactly how I wanted it, even though Mum never stopped moaning. Pictures of David Beckham everywhere, and my Manchester United Number 7 shirt hanging on the wall. Beckham was my hero. OK, I know what you're thinking. Yes, he's gorgeous. You'd have to be blind not to see it. But that's not why I like him. He's a god on the football pitch. *No-one* can bend a ball like Beckham.

'I'm sick of this wedding, and it hasn't even started yet,' I muttered, staring at the poster of Becks over my bed. I talked to him all the time. Beckham looked back at me as if he understood. He always understood. Nobody else did. Not in this house, anyway. It was just 'football shootball'. I remembered a quote by a famous Liverpool manager that I'd read the other day. *Some people think football's a matter of life and death. It's much more important than that.* That was exactly how I felt.

From *Bend It Like Beckham* by Narinder Dhami

Looking at language

1 Skim read the extract from the beginning to her mother's interruption: *'Mum?! Get out of my fantasy!'*

   a What features of television sports commentary has the writer used in this section? Think about the use of verb tenses, direct speech, colloquial language and technical terms.

   b Discuss this in pairs and then pick out examples from the text and explain how they are used.

Interpreting the meanings

2 Close read the rest of the extract to the end. What is Mrs Bhamra's attitude to football and what do we learn from her about what she thinks the priorities of a girl should be? Pick out evidence from the text to support your views.

3 Compare Jess's and her family's attitude towards both football and the family wedding.

In this poem, by Florence McNeil, the narrator, an eleven-year-old, describes the moments just before and after making a dive from a diving board for the first time.

First dive

Shivering in the hot August sun
I stand on the lowest diving board
watching above me the giants
fearlessly twist and knife
into their dark waters

I measure distance
in terms of
multiple whales
and weigh my eleven years
against the terrors
circulating quietly and steadily
under the surface
the eyes that stare from green rocks
at my naked feet
the hands weaving seaweed nets
to complete the ambiguity
of my needless capture
a surfeit of teeth and claws gathering
to oversee my fate

Reckless with fear
I become a wavering sigh
a reluctant bird
lose head and hands and atmosphere
to trespass suddenly
into adult depths
bobbing up transfigured victorious
out of an unclaimed ocean.

By Florence McNeil

Explaining the ideas

1 a Close read the poem in pairs and practise reading it aloud to get a sense of the rhythm. Think about how you are able to **hear the narrator's voice**.

b With your partner identify how the verses take us through the stages of the dive.

Looking at language

2 Scan the poem and discuss how the poet describes the contrast between the narrator and other divers. Make a list of the words in the poem which show the contrast and explain how we know the narrator is an inexperienced diver.

3 How does the poet use language to make the water and the surroundings sound threatening and terrifying to the narrator? Choose three examples from the poem and explain what you think they mean. The first example is given for you:

- *'the terrors circulating quietly and steadily under the surface'*

4 How does the language of the final verse suggest the narrator's sense of achievement?

Discuss with your partner the meaning of the following quotations:

a *I become a wavering sigh*
a reluctant bird

b *bobbing up transfigured victorious*
out of an unclaimed ocean

 Compare

You are now going to compare the ways the writers convey how the characters in each extract feel about 'sport' and the challenges that they face.

1 Firstly consider the challenges faced by all three characters. Discuss with a partner the similarities and differences between the obstacles they face. Record your findings in bullet points under the heading 'Obstacles to success'.

2 Now think about how the writers use language to convey the powerful feelings of the characters towards their sport. Think about the use of:

- description
- colloquial language
- facts and opinions
- figurative language.

In your opinion, which writer conveys the feelings of the character most effectively?

3 Look back at the 'Overcoming adversity' list that you wrote at the start of the unit. Would you now like to add anything to this list?

6 The world of work

Introduction

Earning money for your hard work can be a very satisfying experience, but this has not always been the case. Years ago it was very easy for employers to exploit their work force and it was common for very young children to work for up to 16 hours a day. Nowadays in Britain, there are employment laws which can protect children. However, in some parts of the world, children have to work to support their families and the laws to protect them have yet to be created.

 Text 1 Factory conditions in 1815

 Text 2 We, the working children of the Third World

 Text 3 A passion for print

Reading strategies

- deduce
- read backwards and forwards
- ask questions
- empathise
- establish a relationship with the writer
- rationalise what is happening
- speculate

Pre-reading: empathise

1 Choose two types of job which you think you would enjoy (eg computer programmer, teacher, shop assistant, etc) and two types of job you think you would dislike. List your thoughts about the advantages and disadvantages of each of these jobs.

2 Share your ideas with a partner and then with another pair. Compare similarities and differences in your feelings about the various jobs.

Text 1

The world of work

Factory workers often suffered in appalling conditions in the early nineteenth century. With no employment laws to protect the workers, and stories of dreadful hardship circulating, a Parliamentary Commission was eventually set up to investigate working conditions in factories. This extract, from approximately 1815, contains the evidence given by a young female mill worker named Elizabeth Bentley to the Parliamentary Commissioners.

Factory conditions in 1815

What age are you?
Twenty-three.

Where do you live?
At Leeds.

What time did you begin work at the factory?
When I was six years old.

At whose factory did you work?
Mr Burk's.

What kind of mill is it?
Flax mill.

What was your business in that mill?
I was a little doffer.

What were your hours of labour in that mill?
From 5 in the morning till 9 at night, when they were thronged.[1]

For how long a time together have you worked that excessive length of time?
For about a year.

What were the usual hours of labour when you were not so thronged?
From six in the morning till 7 at night.

What time was allowed for meals?
Forty minutes at noon.

Had you any time to get your breakfast or drinking?
No, we had to get it as we could.

Do you consider doffing a laborious employment?
Yes.

Explain what you had to do.
When the frames are full, they have to stop the frames, and take the flyers off, and take the full bobbins off, and carry them to the roller, and then put empty ones on, and set the frame going again.

Does that keep you constantly on your feet?
Yes, there are so many frames and they run so quick.

[1]thronged – *busy*

Your labour is very excessive?
Yes, you have not time for anything.

Suppose you flagged a little, or were late, what would they do?
Strap us.

And they are in the habit of strapping those who are last in doffing?
Yes.

Constantly?
Yes.

Girls as well as boys?
Yes.

Have you ever been strapped?
Yes.

Severely?
Yes.

Is the strap used so as to hurt you excessively?
Yes it is … I have seen the overlooker go to the top end of the room, where the little girls hug the can to the backminders; he has taken a strap, and a whistle in his mouth, and sometimes he has got a chain and chained them, and strapped them all down the room.

What was his reason for that?
He was very angry.

Did you live far from the mill?
Yes, two miles.

Had you a clock?
No, we had not.

Were you generally there in time?
Yes, my mother has been up at 4 o'clock in the morning, and at 2 o'clock in the morning; the colliers used to go to their work at 3 or 4 o'clock, and when she heard them stirring she has got up out of her warm bed, and gone out and asked them the time; and I have sometimes been at Hunslet Car at 2 o'clock in the morning, when it was streaming down with rain, and we have had to stay till the mill was opened.

You are considerably deformed in person as a consequence of this labour?
Yes I am.

And what time did it come on?
I was about 13 years old when it began coming, and it has got worse since; it is five years since my mother died, and my mother was never able to get me a good pair of stays to hold me up, and when my mother died I had to do for myself, and got me a pair.

Were you perfectly straight and healthy before you worked at a mill?
Yes, I was as straight a little girl as ever went up and down town.

Were you straight till you were 13?
Yes, I was.

Did your deformity come upon you with much pain and weariness?
Yes, I cannot express the pain all the time it was coming.

Do you know of anybody that has been similarly injured in their health?
Yes, in their health, but not many deformed as I am.

It is very common to have weak ankles and crooked knees?
Yes, very common indeed.

This is brought on by stopping the spindle?
Yes.

Where are you now?
In the poorhouse.

State what you think as to the circumstances in which you have been placed during all this time of labour, and what you have considered about it as to the hardship and cruelty of it.
The witness was too much affected to answer the question.

From *Parliamentary Commissioners evidence 1815*

Interpreting the meanings

1 a Find evidence in the text for the poor conditions which Elizabeth Bentley experienced working in the mill. You may find evidence regarding:

- her duties as a 'doffer'
- the significant timings of her day
- rules and discipline
- her health.

b Using this information, **empathise** with her employer and try to justify these conditions. In pairs, role play an interview between the Parliamentary Commissioner and the factory employer. For example you might start:

Q Why did you make your employees work for 16 hours a day?

A I've got orders for cloth to be made and would employ my workers for 24 hours a day if I could. The looms have got to keep going. It's too expensive to shut them down. It costs me money!

The text in its time and place

2 With a partner, create a list of all the things Elizabeth Bentley had to suffer which modern workers would not tolerate. Discuss with your teacher the reasons why Elizabeth had to put up with these conditions.

Looking at language

3 Skim the text to find the following examples of nineteenth-century words and expressions from the text. Try to work out what they might mean. **Read backwards and forwards** to help you.

- a little doffer
- the overlooker
- hug the can to the backminders
- a good pair of stays.

Text 2

The world of work

In some countries, children still have to work from a very young age. Some of these working children have started to organise themselves. They want protection from exploitation but also the opportunity to continue working. The first international conference for working children was held in 1996 and was attended by child workers from 33 countries. Here they formulated the following demands and submitted a poem from one of their members.

'We, the working children of the Third World, propose ...'

1   We want recognition of our problems, our initiatives, proposals and our process of organisation.

2   We are against the boycott of products made by children.

3   We want respect and security for ourselves and the work that we do.

4   We want an education system whose methodology and content are adapted to our reality.

5   We want professional training adapted to our reality and capabilities.

6   We want access to good healthcare for working children.

7   We want to be consulted on all decisions concerning us, at local, national or international level.

8   We want the root causes of our situation, primarily poverty, to be addressed and tackled.

9   We want more activity in rural areas so that children do not have to migrate to the cities.

10 We are against exploitation at work but we are for work with dignity, with hours adapted so that we have time for education and leisure.

In any conference we want representation on an equal basis (if there are 20 ministers present, we want 20 working children also to be present). We will have discussions with our ministers but we do not want them to represent us.

continued

continued

Young daughter of Mali

It is through working that we gain our dignity
It nourishes our survival, our future
What will become of us without work?
A generation of parasites!

Working children,
let us take action in our work
and generate the hopes of future working children.
Working children,
let us persevere in the work we do,
for the future of our country, our environment,
our family and the people we are.
Rise up, working children,
walk hand in hand
and together we will build our future and toil
for the development of all our countries.

From *New Internationalist Magazine*

Explaining the ideas

1   In your own words, summarise the ten things that the working children want.

Looking at language

2   **Try to establish a relationship with the writers** of the text. How do they persuade
you to listen and to take notice of their demands? Think about the tone of their
demands and the language that is used.

3   Read the poem 'Young daughter of Mali' and consider the effect of the following
persuasive techniques used by the writer:

- the opening statement
- use of pronouns – 'we' and 'us'
- use of a rhetorical question and exclamation mark
- use of repetition
- use of verbs such as *'let us'*, *'rise up'* and *'walk hand in hand'*
- use of metaphorical language such as *'nourishes our
  survival'*, *'generation of parasites'* and *'build our future'*.

What is the overall effect? How does the poem differ
from the ten demands?

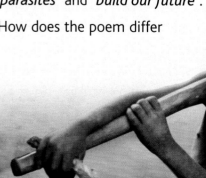

Text 3

The world of work

Have you ever had a part-time job like a paper round? If so, what would you say you learned about the world of work from your experiences? In his autobiography *The Road to Nab End*, William Woodruff describes his early working experiences as a newspaper delivery boy in Lancashire in the 1920s.

A passion for print

While we were living at Livingstone Road I really began to earn my keep. I took pride in doing so. I started delivering morning and evening newspapers for George and Madge Latham, a young, childless couple in their thirties, who ran a sweets, tobacco and newspaper business on Revidge Road. The Lathams were an honest, hard-working couple. They were Lancashire folk: active, tough, resourceful. They were always cheerful. I was a year below the minimum age, but they took me on just the same; no one enforced the law. They paid me the princely sum of two shillings and sixpence per week, of which I kept a dodger. Mother took the rest. That was my contribution to help pay for the house.

I came to spend so much time with the Lathams that home and school fell into the background. Winter and summer, wet or fine, I got myself up at five to meet George at the newspaper depot in the centre of town about a mile and a half away. I had to run through the dark, hushed streets for half an hour or so. I'd find him waiting for me with his bicycle. On cold mornings his teeth were chattering. Together, we then fought our way in and out of an ill-lit warehouse that served as the newspaper depot. It was a daily hand-to-hand battle with other men to get our newspapers. It was bedlam there.

Once we'd got the warm, damp bundles under our arms, we loaded them and George's bike onto the first tram to Revidge Road at six o'clock. Kneeling on the ribbed floor, we sorted the papers as the tram lurched along. When the floor was wet with melted snow off people's clogs, we used the seats. At Revidge Road, George helped me off the tram. With a bag of newspapers on either shoulder, I began my round. Depending on the weather, I'd be running through the streets for the next hour, or hour and a half. I found it wonderful to have the world to myself.

continued ▶

continued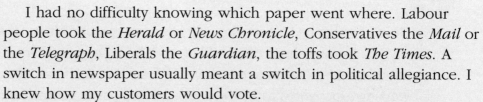

I had no difficulty knowing which paper went where. Labour people took the *Herald* or *News Chronicle*, Conservatives the *Mail* or the *Telegraph*, Liberals the *Guardian*, the toffs took *The Times*. A switch in newspaper usually meant a switch in political allegiance. I knew how my customers would vote.

Delivering newspapers taught me a lot about human nature. I learned to recognise the news addicts and the insomniacs. In summer, these chaps paced up and down their lawns awaiting my arrival. The way they snatched the paper out of my hand, made me feel important. I knew by the way they rushed to the financial pages that, like most of the rich, they were fearful of losing their money. I'd nothing to lose so the financial crashes left me unmoved. I decided it must be worrying to be rich.

In bad weather, the kind-hearted awaited my arrival with a cup of tea and a bun. The not so kind angrily waved the paper in my face as if I were responsible for the success of Labour at the polls, or the assassination of the head of a foreign state. I felt like saying: 'Look, Mister, I don't write these papers, I just deliver them.' Usually, I kept my mouth shut. One thing I did learn was never to give a man the wrong paper. You've no idea how touchy some people can be. They'd bawl me out as if I'd permanently committed them to the wrong religion.

In time I came to have a large family of newspaper readers. I knew them more closely than they realised. I knew them by the way their houses stared, sat and slept. I closely followed my customers' births, weddings, divorces and deaths. I knew who had gone broke, and who was doing very nicely. I knew when a move was under way. I delivered Dr Michael's paper. He was the great ear, nose and throat specialist who was unable to save his own daughter from a fatal ear infection. 'And how is the Michael child?' some customers asked me as if I were a consulting physician.

With a passion for the printed word, I not only delivered newspapers, I read them too. I started every day eager to see what the world was up to.

One thing I did learn, was the way newspapers contradicted each other – that truth is not as straight-forward as I thought it was. A disaster in politics in one paper was a victory in another. I asked myself how could that be? I also learned to be suspicious of the writers who had a simple answer for everything. Every day I read the column by Hannan Swaffer in the *Daily Herald*. Why, if they'd have put Mr Swaffer in charge, the country and the world would have been on its feet again in seven days. I found it confusing.

I asked George Latham what he made of it; after all, he had newsprint all over his hands as I did, and he was much older.

'I'd never deliver the news, Billy, if I tried to make head or tail of it,' he answered. 'We're businessmen, Billy. We have our work cut out delivering papers without worrying about what it all means.'

From *The Road to Nab End* by William Woodruff

Interpreting the meanings

1   Close read the three paragraphs from *'Delivering newspapers taught me a lot about human nature…'* to *'…as if I were a consulting physician.'*

   a   Create a bullet point list of the things William Woodruff learned on his paper round. What do these points help you to **deduce** about the young William's personality? Create a table like the one below:

Information from the text	What it tells us about the writer
• 'I learned to recognise the news addicts and the insomniacs'	• He is observant. He distinguishes the differences between his customers.
•	•
•	•

What the writer thinks

2   Imagine that William Woodruff is being interviewed on the radio about his experiences as a newspaper delivery boy. In pairs, write a list of **questions that can be asked** which will bring out the writer's feelings, views and attitudes towards the work. Then role play the interview. The person playing William Woodruff will need to **speculate** about what his responses will be.

Compare

You are going to choose two of the texts and write an essay comparing the ways in which they deal with 'The world of work'.

First consider the following points and make notes about each text as you work through them.

1 Think about the ways in which the young people in the texts are treated.

   a Which texts give the most details about working conditions?

   b Which texts deal directly with the young people's feelings?

   c Compare the feelings about work expressed in the texts.

2 In Elizabeth Bentley's testimony, the text is written in a question and answer layout.

   a How does this make the reader feel as they read the text?

   b Compare this layout with the other two texts. Do the different layouts affect your feelings as a reader?

3 How do the writers use language to express their ideas? Think about:

- the type of information chosen
- the length and types of sentences
- the amount of detail included
- the use of colloquial expressions and more formal language.

4 Each text deals with only one viewpoint.

   a Explain what the different viewpoints are.

   b In your opinion, which text expresses the young person's viewpoint most powerfully?

5 Now choose two of the texts for your comparative essay. Don't forget to explain how the texts achieve their effects, and support your points with precise references to the text. Plan your response with care before you write.

7 Discoveries

Introduction

For all of us there are moments in our lives when we discover something for the first time. Sometimes it can be something we have worked hard towards and at other times it can be a spontaneous experience. The texts you are going to read in this unit all explore the emotions and excitement of these moments of discovery.

 Text 1 My first oyster   **Text 2** Educating Rita   **Text 3** The colour of radium

Reading strategies

● hear a reading voice   ● ask questions   ● infer   ● deduce   ● feel

Pre-reading: feel

1 Working in pairs, share a moment from your past when you discovered something for the first time. Make a list of the feelings you had and then comment on how influential or important the moment was in your life.

2 Think of three famous people you have read about who have made a great discovery. For example, the scientist Isaac Newton was hit on the head by an apple which led him to discover the theory of gravity. Make a list of the different feelings which these people would have had and discuss them with your partner.

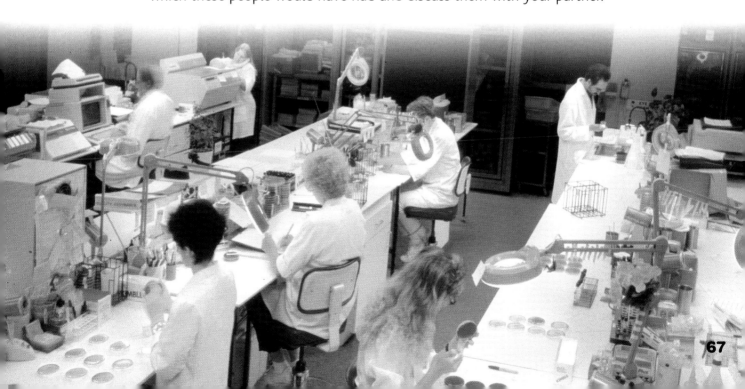

Discoveries

This text is from an autobiographical account of his life by the chef, Anthony Bourdain. In this extract the writer recalls the moment when he ate an oyster for the first time and discovered the joy of food, an event that would influence his choice of career as a chef.

My first oyster

When our neighbor, Monsieur Saint-Jour, the oyster fisherman, invited my family out on his *pinasse* (oyster boat), I was enthusiastic.

At six in the morning, we boarded Monsieur Saint-Jour's small wooden vessel with our picnic baskets and our sensible footwear. He was a crusty old fellow, dressed like my uncle in ancient denim coveralls, espadrilles and beret. He had a leathery, tanned and windblown face, hollow cheeks, and the tiny broken blood vessels on nose and cheeks that everyone seemed to have. He hadn't fully briefed his guests on what was involved in these daily trips. We put-putted out to a buoy marking his underwater oyster *parc*, a fenced-off section of bay bottom, and we sat ... and sat ... and sat, in the roaring August sun, waiting for the tide to go out. The idea was to float the boat over the stockaded fence walls, then sit there until the boat slowly sank with the water level, until it rested on the *bassin* floor. At this point, Monsieur Saint-Jour, and his guests presumably, would rake the oysters, collect a few good specimens for sale in port, and remove any parasites that might be endangering his crop.

There was, I recall, still about two feet of water left to go before the hull of the boat settled on dry ground and we could walk about the *parc*. We'd already polished off the Brie and baguettes and downed the Evian, but I was still hungry, and characteristically said so.

Monsieur Saint-Jour, on hearing this – as if challenging his American passengers – inquired in his thick Girondais accent, if any of us would care to try an oyster.

My parents hesitated. I doubt they'd realized they might actually have to *eat* one of the raw, slimy things we were currently floating over. My little brother recoiled in horror.

But I, in the proudest moment of my young life, stood up smartly, grinning with defiance, and volunteered to be the first.

And in that unforgettably sweet moment in my personal history, that one moment still more alive for me than so many of the other 'firsts' which followed – first day in high school, first published book, or any other first thing – I attained glory. Monsieur Saint-Jour beckoned me over to the gunwale, where he leaned over, reached down until his head nearly disappeared underwater, and emerged holding a single silt-encrusted oyster, huge and irregularly shaped, in his rough, clawlike fist. With a snubby, rust-covered oyster knife, he popped the thing open and handed it to me, everyone watching now, my little brother shrinking away from this glistening object, still dripping and nearly alive.

I took it in my hand, tilted the shell back into my mouth as instructed by the now beaming Monsieur Saint-Jour, and with one bite and a slurp, wolfed it down. It tasted of seawater ... of brine and flesh ... and somehow ... of the future.

Everything was different now. Everything.

I'd not only survived – I'd *enjoyed*.

This, I knew, was the magic I had until now been only dimly and spitefully aware of. I was hooked. My parents' shudders, my little brother's expression of unrestrained revulsion and amazement only reinforced the sense that I had, somehow, become a man. I had had an *adventure*, and everything that followed in my life would all stem from this moment.

I'd learned something. And there was no turning back. Food had *power*. It could inspire, astonish, shock, excite, delight and impress. It had the power to please me ... and others. My life as a cook, and as a chef, had begun.

From *Kitchen Confidential* by Anthony Bourdain

Interpreting the meanings

1 Skim read the text from the beginning to '... *still dripping and nearly alive'* at the end of paragraph seven.

  a How does the writer describe Monsieur Saint-Jour? What can you **deduce** about what he thinks of his guests?

  b In paragraph six, the writer describes himself as *'grinning with defiance'* at this moment. What can you **infer** from this about his attitude to his family?

Looking at language

2 Scan paragraph seven. How does the writer use language to make it clear to the reader that this was an *'unforgettably sweet'* moment? Think about the use of emotive verbs, noun phrases and adverbials.

What the writer thinks

3 Close read the text from *'I took it in my hand'* to the end of the text. How does the writer show that eating the oyster changes his life completely at this point?

Discoveries

This text is taken from a play about Rita, a hairdresser from Liverpool who decides to do a university degree against the wishes of her husband and family. In this extract Rita has been to see a play by Shakespeare for the first time and describes her reactions to the play to her university tutor, Frank.

Educating Rita

Rita *bursts through the door out of breath*

Frank What are you doing here? *(He looks at his watch)* It's Thursday, you ...

Rita *(moving over to the desk, quickly)* I know I shouldn't be here, it's me dinner hour, but listen, I've gorra tell someone, have y' got a few minutes, can y' spare ...?

Frank *(alarmed) My* God, what is it?

Rita I had to come an' tell y', Frank, last night, I went to the theatre! A proper one, a professional theatre.

Frank *(sighing)* For God's sake, you had me worried, I thought it was something serious.

Rita No, listen, it was. I went out an' got me ticket, it was Shakespeare, I thought it was gonna be dead borin' ...

Frank Then why did you go in the first place?

Rita I wanted to find out. But listen, it wasn't borin', it was bleedin' great, honest, ogh, it done me in, it was fantastic. I'm gonna do an essay on it.

Frank *(smiling)* Come on, which one was it?

Rita *moves* UP RIGHT CENTRE

Rita '... Out; out, brief candle!
Life's but a walking shadow, a poor player
That struts and frets his hour upon the stage
And then is heard no more. It is a tale
Told by an idiot, full of sound and fury
Signifying nothing.'

Frank *(deliberately)* Ah, *Romeo and Juliet.*

Rita *(moving towards* **Frank***)* Tch. Frank! Be serious. I learnt that
today from the book. *(She produces a copy of 'Macbeth')* Look, I went
out an' bought the book. Isn't it great? What I couldn't get over is how
excitin' it was.

Frank *puts his feet up on the desk*

Rita Wasn't his wife a cow, eh? An' that fantastic bit where he
meets Macduff an' he thinks he's all invincible. I was on the edge of me
seat at that bit. I wanted to shout out an' tell Macbeth, warn him.

Frank You didn't, did you?

Rita Nah. Y' can't do that in a theatre, can y'? It was dead good. It
was like a thriller.

Frank Yes. You'll have to go and see more.

Rita I'm goin' to. Macbeth's a tragedy, isn't it?

Frank *nods*

Rita Right.

Rita *smiles at* **Frank** *and he smiles back at her* Well I just – I just
had to tell someone who'd understand.

Frank I'm honoured that you chose me.

Rita *(moving towards the door)* Well, I better get back. I've left a
customer with a perm lotion. If I don't get a move on there'll be another
tragedy.

Frank No. There won't be a tragedy.

Rita There will, y'know. I know this woman; she's dead fussy. If her
perm doesn't come out right there'll be blood an' guts everywhere.

Frank Which might be quite tragic –
He throws her the apple from his desk which she catches
– but it won't be a tragedy.

Rita What?

Frank Well – erm – look; the tragedy of the drama has nothing to
do with the sort of tragic event you're talking about. Macbeth is flawed
by his ambition – yes?

Rita *(going and sitting in the chair by the desk)* Yeh. Go on.
(She starts to eat the apple)

Frank Erm – it's that flaw which forces him to take the inevitable
steps towards his own doom. You see?

Rita *offers him the can of soft drink. He takes it and looks at it*

Frank *(putting the can down on the desk)* No thanks. Whereas,
Rita, a woman's hair being reduced to an inch of stubble, or –
or the sort of thing you read in the paper that's reported as
being tragic, 'Man Killed By Falling Tree', is not a tragedy.

continued

continued

Rita It is for the poor sod under the tree.

Frank Yes, it's tragic, absolutely tragic. But it's not a tragedy in the way that *Macbeth* is a tragedy. Tragedy in dramatic terms is inevitable, pre-ordained. Look, now, even without ever having heard the story of *Macbeth* you wanted to shout out, to warn him and prevent him going on, didn't you? But you wouldn't have been able to stop him would you?

Rita No.

Frank Why?

Rita They would have thrown me out the theatre.

Frank But what I mean is that your warning would have been ignored. He's warned in the play. But he can't go back. He still treads the path to doom. But the poor old fellow under the tree hasn't arrived there by following any inevitable steps has he?

Rita No.

Frank There's no particular flaw in his character that has dictated his end. If he'd been warned of the consequences of standing beneath that particular tree he wouldn't have done it, would he? Understand.

Rita So – so Macbeth brings it on himself?

Frank Yes. You see he goes blindly on and on and with every step he's spinning one more piece of thread which will eventually make up the network of his own tragedy. Do you see?

Rita I think so. I'm not used to thinkin' like this.

Frank It's quite easy, Rita.

Rita It is for you. I just thought it was a dead excitin' story. But the way you tell it you make me see all sorts of things in it. (*After a pause*) It's fun, tragedy, isn't it?

From *Educating Rita* by Willy Russell

Looking at language

1   Skim read the text from the beginning to '*I'm honoured that you chose me.*' What does Rita find so '*fantastic*' about the production of Macbeth that she has just seen? Make a list of the details that she comments on.

2   Close read the text to the end. How does the writer make the discussion about tragedy amusing? Find three quotations and explain why the audience would find them funny.

3   With a partner, read the text aloud from '*Well, I better get back ...*' to the end.

   a   How do the stage directions and the different language used by Rita and Frank help you to understand what the characters are like?

   b   **Ask questions** of the text and then make two spider diagrams recording your ideas about each character. Support your points with quotations from the text.

Discoveries

This text is from a biography of the scientist, Marie Curie, by her daughter Eve. Here, the writer paints a vivid picture of Marie and Pierre Curie's obsession with their discovery of a new radioactive element, radium.

The colour of radium

It was nine o'clock at night. Pierre and Marie Curie were in their little house at 108 Boulevard Kellermann, where they had been living since 1900.

Old Dr Curie, who lived with the couple, had retired to his room. Marie had bathed her child and put her to bed, and had stayed for a long time beside the cot. This was a rite. When Irène did not feel her mother near her at night she would call out for her incessantly. And Marie, yielding to the implacability of the four-year-old child, climbed the stairs, seated herself beside her and stayed there in the darkness until the young voice gave way to light, regular breathing. Only then would she go down again to Pierre, who was growing impatient. In spite of his kindness, he was the most possessive and jealous of husbands. He was so used to the constant presence of his wife that her least eclipse kept him from thinking freely. If Marie delayed too long near her daughter, he received her on her return with a reproach so unjust as to be comic:

'You never think of anything but that child!'

Pierre walked slowly about the room. Marie sat down and made some stitches on the hem of Irène's new apron. But this evening she could not fix her attention. Nervous, she got up; then, suddenly:

'Suppose we go down there for a moment?'

There was a note of supplication[1] in her voice – altogether superfluous[2], for Pierre, like herself, longed to go back to the shed they had left two hours before. Radium, fanciful as a living creature, endearing as a love, called them back to its dwelling, to the wretched laboratory. The day's work had been hard, and it would have been more reasonable for the couple to rest. But Pierre and Marie were not always reasonable. As soon as they had put on their coats and told Dr Curie of their flight, they were in the street. They went on foot, arm in arm, exchanging few words. After the crowded streets of this queer district, with its factory buildings, wastelands and

[1]supplication – *asking humbly*
[2]superfluous – *unnecessary*

continued

continued poor tenements, they arrived in the Rue Lhomond and crossed the little courtyard. Pierre put the key in the lock. The door squeaked, as it had squeaked thousands of times, and admitted them to their realm, to their dream.

'Don't light the lamps!' Marie said in the darkness. Then she added with a little laugh:

'Do you remember the day when you said to me: "I should like radium to have a beautiful colour"?'

The reality was more entrancing than the simple wish of long ago. Radium had something better than 'a beautiful colour'; it was spontaneously luminous. And in the sombre shed, where, in the absence of cupboards, the precious particles in their tiny glass receivers were placed on tables or on shelves nailed to the wall, their phosphorescent bluish outlines gleamed, suspended in the night.

'Look ... Look!' the young woman murmured.

She went forward cautiously, looked for and found a straw-bottomed chair. She sat down in the darkness and silence. Their two faces turned toward the pale glimmering, the mysterious sources of radiation, toward radium – their radium. Her body leaning forward, her head eager, Marie took up again the attitude which had been hers an hour earlier at the bedside of her sleeping child. Her companion's hand lightly touched her hair. She was to remember for ever this evening of glow-worms, this magic.

From *Marie Curie* by Eve Curie (translated by Vincent Sheean)

Looking at language

1   Skim read the text. **Infer** and **deduce** to pick out words and phrases that show that Pierre and Marie's scientific work is of great importance to them.

2   The writer uses language to describe radium and help the reader to understand what an amazing discovery it was. Copy and complete the following table. Pick out the words and phrases used to describe radium and explain their effect on the reader. The first example and explanation is done for you.

Quotation	Explanation
'Fanciful as a living creature'	Simile comparing radium's unpredictable nature to a living thing. Makes the reader feel that Marie Curie needs to watch it closely.

Compare

You are now going to compare the ways different writers use language and form to convey powerful experiences

1   Look again at Text 2: Educating Rita and one of the other texts.

   a   Compare the feelings of two of the characters about their moment of discovery. Discuss your findings with a partner and make notes under the name of each of your chosen characters. Then look closely at the language used by the writers to describe:

   •   the feelings of the chosen characters

   •   the feelings of other characters

   •   what each character learns or gains from his or her moment of discovery.

   b   In your pairs compare the effects of the two texts on the reader. Make notes under the heading of each text and consider the following:

   •   the form in which the text is presented (eg playscript, information text, autobiography, biography)

   •   the techniques a dramatic text uses to convey meaning. How do these differ from the other text?

   •   the place of the writer in relation to the reader. How are we directly or indirectly involved by the writer?

3   Choose one short piece from each text which appealed to you or which you found particularly effective.

   a   Compare your examples with a partner's and discuss why you have chosen them.

   b   Prepare a short presentation and present your views to the rest of the class.

8 Rituals

Introduction

Rituals are like customs and play an important part in many different cultures. They are sometimes associated with religion; for example, in Christian cultures it is the custom to celebrate the birth of Jesus. In Britain, this custom or ritual is called Christmas. Rituals can also symbolise a rite of passage, for example, the celebration of a birth or marriage. The texts in this unit look at different types of rituals and explore how they influence people's relationships with friends, family or the wider community.

 The walk of death

 Preparations for marriage

 How do Buddhists worship?

Reading strategies

- relate to your own experience
- speculate
- ask questions
- predict what will happen
- empathise
- infer

Pre-reading: ask questions

1 Can you think of any rituals that are particularly important to the society that you live in or a culture that you are familiar with? The rituals could be to do with friends, groups that you belong to, family, your culture or religion. Record your ideas on a table, describing the ritual and why it is important.

2 Share your ideas with a partner. Did you choose the same or a different ritual? What did you find interesting about the ritual your partner described? Think of a list of further **questions you would like to ask** to find out more information.

3 Now contribute to a class discussion on the importance of rituals. Do you think rituals are important? Discuss the positive benefits that rituals can have.

Rituals

This is an extract from the novel *Tribes* written by Catherine MacPhail. In this extract, Kevin wants to join a gang called the Tribe, but before Doc, Torry and Salom allow him to join their gang he has to complete an initiation test to prove his bravery.

The walk of death

It was an ugly old building, red brick, with every window smashed and half the inside missing. At night, whenever Kevin would pass those broken windows, they reminded him of sunken skeleton eyes. Now, as they approached it in the twilight, it looked even scarier. He had often imagined how terrifying it would be to be trapped in there in the dark. Now, with a shudder, he had a feeling that was going to be his fate.

'Is that where we're going?' he asked.

Salom grinned. 'That's where we're going.'

Kevin felt his pulse quicken and his heart began to beat faster.

He had a notion to run then but, at that moment, Salom slipped an arm around his shoulder, friendly, yet very firm, leading him inside the gaping mouth of that redbrick monster.

'Come, my friend,' he said. 'There's no turning back now.'

It was really dark inside the building, but Kevin wasn't given a chance for his eyes to become accustomed to the blackness. Doc pulled a scarf from his jacket pocket.

'What are you going to do with that?' Kevin asked him.

'Blindfold you,' Doc said stonily.

'What? Are you not going to let me see what I'm doing?'

Maybe they *were* going to make him eat something awful, then guess what it was.

Doc tied the blindfold roughly round his eyes. This boy didn't like Kevin, that was for sure.

'If you're going to tie me up here all night,' Kevin said, trying to sound as if the thought didn't bother him at all, 'someone will have to tell my parents I'm staying over with them.'

Again it was Doc who answered sarcastically. 'You think it's going to be that simple? Stay the night in the old dark warehouse?'

'That's kids' stuff,' Torry said.

'You'll soon know what it is, Kev,' Salom said, at the same time guiding him gently. 'Be careful. We're going up the stairs.'

Going up. That phrase scared him too. Kevin was scared of heights, always had been. He could visualize the stairs in this old building.

continued

continued

Broken, crumbling, dangerous. And he was going up them, blindfolded. This had to be the daftest thing he'd ever done.

Step by faltering step he climbed, held gently but firmly by Salom, who encouraged him in his soft voice. 'One more step here, Kev. Now we're turning. Almost there.'

Sometimes a hand would push him roughly forward. He knew who that belonged to – Doc, pushing him so hard he almost tripped.

And he could hear Torry skipping up the stairs behind him, laughing. Looking forward to what was ahead.

What was ahead? How high were they going? It seemed to Kevin that they had been climbing for ever.

He was breathing hard. But it wasn't from the climb. He knew that. It was nerves.

But where was he going?

He could hear faint traffic noises far below.

Far below.

How far?

He tried to remember how many storeys this warehouse had. Seven? Eight? He'd never counted, in all the times he'd passed here and looked up. Now he wished he had.

They came to a final step and, as Salom turned him on to a landing, Kevin felt a gust of cold night air from a broken window.

'We're here,' Salom said, turning Kevin towards him. 'Doc, take off the blindfold.'

As roughly as he had put it on, Doe whipped it off.

Kevin blinked. It took a few seconds for his eyes to grow accustomed to the darkness. And it was dark now. No moon. No stars. A cloudy sky overhead.

He looked around him. They were high in the building, not quite on the top floor, but near enough. Dust and broken glass lay everywhere. Behind him, the crumbling stairs he had just climbed. In front of him ...

Kevin gasped and stepped back. In front of him was nothing. He was standing at the edge of a gaping chasm, a hole that stretched to nothingness below. At the other side of that chasm, it looked a million miles away, was a minute stretch of floor and a smashed window. And all that connected the floor Kevin was standing on to that other side was a narrow wooden beam. Kevin looked at Torry. He was smiling, his hands on his hips. He looked at Doc. There was something malevolent in his eyes. And then he looked at Salom. He stepped on to the beam like an acrobat. Kevin gasped.

Salom grinned. 'You get to the other side, and you are a fully paid-up member of the Tribe.'

They couldn't be serious. They expected him to cross over there. Below him, a sheer drop? No way!

Salom stepped back and gestured to the beam, like a magician. 'Welcome,' he said, 'to the Walk of Death.'

From *Tribes* by Catherine MacPhail

Interpreting the meanings

1   Close read the text. **Speculate** on why the group call themselves the 'Tribe'.

2   **a**   Find evidence from the text to contrast Doc's and Salom's attitude towards Kevin joining the 'Tribe'. You will need to **infer**. Record your evidence on a table like the one below:

Doc's attitude	What it implies	Salom's attitude	What it implies
'Doc tied the blindfold roughly'	Doc doesn't mind if he hurts Kevin	'Salom slipped an arm around his shoulder, friendly, yet very firm'	Salom is supportive towards Kevin

   b   Why do you think that Doc might be behaving in this way?

   c   Why do you think that Salom seems keen for Kevin to join the 'Tribe'?

Looking at language

3   How does the writer build up tension in this text? Comment on:

   • Kevin's growing anxiety
   • how the others prepare him for the test
   • how the writer appeals to our senses
   • Kevin's reaction to the test.

4   How would you feel in Kevin's situation? **Empathise**. What would you do? Will Kevin meet the challenge? **Predict what will happen** next.

Rituals

This is an extract from the fantasy novel *Slaves of the Mastery* by William Nicholson. In this text, a young woman, Sisi, and her mother, the Johdi, are preparing for Sisi's forthcoming marriage. In Sisi's culture it is customary for the bride not to choose her husband but to allow her parents to make the choice. Here, Sisi is keen to find out about her mother's feelings and attitudes towards marriage.

Preparations for marriage

Meanwhile the Johdi was rehearsing her daughter in the wedding ceremony. It was many years since she had performed the five steps herself, but she remembered every moment vividly.

'My mother cried all through my wedding day. I shall cry, I know it. Now the most important thing to remember is to keep the steps small. Like this.'

The Johdi shuffled forward, one small step.

'Remember, every time you step forward, he steps forward. You don't want to bump into him. I've known weddings where they never had room for the fifth step. And you know what that means.'

'No, mama, What does it mean?'

'One of you will die ten years before the other. Each step stands for ten years together. So let's practise. I'll be the man.'

They stood facing each other at opposite ends of the main saloon of the royal carriage.

'Hands clasped. Look down.' Sisi did as she was told. 'He moves, then you move. There. Now you.'

Sisi stepped forward.

'Pause. There'll be music. Don't look up until after the third step.'

'Why am I not to look up?'

'In the early years, a good wife is ruled by her husband.'

'But you're not ruled by papa.'

'Only in the early years, darling. Now I step. And off you go again.'

Sisi stepped forward.

'Before you were married, mama, did you want to be married to papa?'

'Of course I did, darling. He was the son of the Johanna of Gang. The old Johanna, that is.'

'But did you love him?'

'Now the third step. How could I possibly love him, dear? You can't love a man if you've never so much as said good morning to him.'

'What if you hadn't liked him?'

'Fourth step. Keep it small.'

Sisi stepped forward.

'Now look up. Keep your head up from now on.'

Sisi looked up at her mother. She was close now.

'I chose to like him. As you will do. Fifth step.'

The Johdi stepped forward, and Sisi followed. Now they were close enough to touch. Her mother parted her plump hands and declared,

'With these five steps, I stand before you as your husband. Do you receive me as my wife?'

'And all I say is, yes?'

'You say yes, my darling. And you're a wife.'

Sisi felt a great sadness come over her. Not wanting her mother to see, she put her arms round her and buried her face in the Johdi's ample bosom.

'There, my sweet one. There, there.'

'Mama,' said Sisi after a moment. 'Have you been happy, married to papa?'

The Johdi sighed.

'I know no other life,' she said. 'He's a good man. Who's to say it would have been any better with anyone else?'

From *Slaves of the Mastery* by William Nicholson

Interpreting the meanings

1 Close read the text and try to **empathise** with Sisi. What particular aspects of the marriage is she anxious about? Select words and phrases from the text to support your argument.

2 Scan the text. Find words or phrases that show Sisi's mother's feelings about marriage. Explain what they reveal about her attitude towards marriage. The first example is completed for you:

Evidence from the text	Her attitude
'You can't love a man if you've never so much as said good morning to him'	She did not expect to have the opportunity to get to know her husband or love him before marriage

3 Scan the text again. Pick out evidence of any rituals surrounding marriage. What do you think the five steps represent? Discuss your ideas with a partner and then share them with the rest of the group.

Text 3 Rituals

Buddhism is a religion that began in India in the sixth century BC. Buddhists believe that happiness can be achieved only if we get rid of all our selfish desires. Today there are 360 million Buddhist worshippers worldwide. This text is taken from an information book, *What do we know about Buddhism?*, and aims to answer some of the questions the reader might have about the rituals and symbols surrounding Buddhism.

HOW DO BUDDHISTS WORSHIP?

When Buddhists visit the temple, they put their hands together in greeting, then kneel and bow three times before the statue of the Buddha or *bodhisattva* in the shrine-room. The three bows are to represent the Buddha, the *dharma* and the *sangha*. Then they offer gifts of flowers, candles, incense and food. The gifts show their respect for the Buddha and their thanks for his teaching. They repeat the Five Precepts and pledge their commitment to the Three Jewels. They may also spend some time meditating, chanting or listening to monks reading from the sacred texts. Buddhists visit the temple whenever they wish, but especially on full moon days and some festivals.

A BUDDHIST CHANT

This is a Buddhist chant from the *Metta Sutta* which encourages kindness and compassion to others:

May all beings be happy,
Whatever they are,
Weak or strong,
Tall, short or medium,
Small or large.
May all without exception
be happy,
Beings seen or unseen,
Those who live near or far away,
Those who are born
And those who are yet to be born.
May all beings be happy.

INSIDE THE TEMPLE

These Buddhists are worshipping in the main shrine-room of the Shwedagon Pagoda in Myanmar. They have taken off their shoes as a mark of respect. The shrine is beautifully decorated, with several golden statues of the Buddha. These statues remind people of the Buddha's good qualities and teaching, and of the possibility of gaining enlightenment by following his example.

TEMPLE OFFERINGS

Worshippers take offerings of candles, flowers and incense to place on the shrine in front of the Buddha. Candles are lit to represent the light offered by the Buddha's teachings which help to get rid of the darkness of ignorance. Flowers look and smell sweet but they wilt and die, a reminder of the teaching that nothing lasts for ever. People chant or say prayers as they make their offerings. They may also leave gifts of food for the monks. Making offerings is believed to be a way of gaining good *karma* and of moving closer to *nirvana*.

PRAYER WHEELS

As she walks around the temple, this Tibetan woman tells her rosary in one hand and spins the huge prayer wheels with the other. A prayer wheel is a cylinder with a paper scroll inside. Thousands of prayers are written on the scroll. By spinning the wheels, she releases the prayers into the world.

Worshippers always walk around holy places in a clockwise direction, spinning the wheels with their right hands. This is because they believe that they should move around the Buddha in the same way as the planets move around the sun. They also repeat the sacred mantra, *Om mani padme hum*, or 'Praise to the jewel in the lotus'.

TIBETAN WORSHIP

The objects shown here are also used as part of Tibetan worship. To the left is a hand-held prayer wheel, which people can spin as they walk. The bell in the middle represents wisdom. It is rung during religious ceremonies. The unusual object on the far right is called a *vajra*. It is the symbol of the Buddha's power and of the truth behind everything.

Prayer wheel   Bell   Vajra

From *What do we know about Buddhism?* by Anita Ganeri

Explaining the ideas

1 a Scan the text and list five rituals that are important in Buddhist worship.

   b Look at the pictures and captions that accompany them. What are the symbols of ritual in Buddhist tradition and what do they represent? Record your ideas, summarising key points in your own words, on a table like the one below:

Ritual	What it represents
Buddhists worship statues of Buddha	The statues remind followers of Buddha to follow his good example

Interpreting the meanings

2 Close read the *Metta Sutta*. How does this Buddhist chant encourage kindness and compassion towards others? **Ask questions** and consider:

   • the viewpoint expressed
   • the language used
   • the use of verbs and adjectives
   • the use of contrasts.

Compare

Compare how the different rituals are presented in Text 1: The walk of death and Text 2: Preparations for marriage.

For each text, consider the questions below. You could record your answers in a table.

1 a What are the rituals that Kevin and Sisi take part in?

   b What do these rituals represent?

   c Do they symbolise anything (eg rite of passage)?

2 a What is it that motivates them to take part in the ritual?

   b Is it their own choice or are they under pressure in any way?

3 a What do the rituals mean in terms of belonging and identity?

   b What would it mean to go through with the ritual?

   c What would happen if they didn't or failed?

4 What are their feelings about taking part in the ritual? Comment on and give reasons for their:
   • anxiety
   • inexperience
   • reluctance.

5 How do the texts explore the ideas of experience versus inexperience?

9 Violent Earth

Introduction

Britain can suffer from bad storms and floods, but our climate is relatively gentle compared with some regions in the world which are regularly subjected to natural disasters, such as earthquakes, hurricanes and volcanoes. These phenomena are a reminder of the power that can be unleashed by natural forces and how vulnerable people are to these destructive events.

 Terror in the harbour   The storm   Hurricane

Reading strategies

- hear a reading voice
- speculate
- make judgements
- see images
- rationalise what is happening
- predict what will happen
- establish a relationship with the writer
- read backwards and forwards

Pre-reading: speculate

1   Have you ever been in the middle of a hurricane, earthquake, volcanic eruption or tidal wave? Television news pictures and newspaper photographs show the reality of these events but leave much to the imagination. With a partner, discuss the likely effects that each of these natural disasters might have on a community:

Natural disaster	Possible effect on the community
Hurricane	
Earthquake	
Volcanic eruption	
Tidal wave	

2   Compare your responses with another pair in your group. Are they much the same? What difference do you think real experience of these natural disasters makes to your ideas?

Violent Earth

Tidal waves or tsunamis have been much exaggerated in fiction and films, but do occur fairly regularly in countries such as Japan. They are generally triggered by undersea earthquakes which generate waves of considerable power. These move towards the coast and can devastate a coastline and wipe out entire communities. This text is a magazine article and explores the phenomenon of tsunamis.

In deep water they pass unnoticed, but as tsunamis approach land the waves rise to tens of metres tall.

Terror in the harbour

Tsunamis are giant sea waves that have nothing to do with tides but everything to do with earthquakes. Most result from large (at least magnitude 6.5 on the Richter Scale), shallow submarine earthquakes that spontaneously jolt thousands of square kilometres of sea bed sending waves rippling out in all directions. One of the extraordinary characteristics of a tsunami is that in deep water it is hardly detectable, and can pass under ships unnoticed. As it approaches land, however, the wave front begins to slow as the seabed shallows and water piles up behind forming a towering wave that can be tens of metres high. This explains why the Japanese term tsunami means 'harbour wave'. Fishermen at sea would not feel the earthquake nor the tsunami, but would return to find their harbours destroyed, their homes washed away and their families dead.

There are many reasons why tsunamis

are such terrifying destroyers. First of all, they are fast. In deep water, a tsunami can travel at more than 800km/h, and can cross an ocean basin as quickly as a jet. Secondly, the distance from crest to crest can be hundreds of kilometres, compared with a few tens of metres for the wind-driven waves that crash on our shores. This means that when a tsunami strikes a coastline, it just keeps coming, perhaps for ten minutes or more, before taking as long to withdraw. The sheer power of a tsunami is also extraordinary, and is sufficient to demolish concrete structures, tear buildings from the ground and batter the life out of humans.

There is no question that tsunamis are killers and, during the 20th century, more than 400 of them have taken 50,000 lives. There is increasing awareness, however, that things may become worse in the future, and concern is growing about so-called mega-tsunamis that are formed not as a result of submarine earthquakes but due to giant landslides from collapsing ocean island volcanoes. Worries are focusing on the Canary Island of La Palma where, during an eruption in 1949 of the Cumbre Vieja volcano, the entire western flank – a mass of rock twice the size of the Isle of Man – dropped by about four metres before grinding to a halt.

Recently, Steve Ward of the University of California at Santa Cruz and Simon Day of University College London raised concern to new levels when they published a model of the tsunamis that would be generated by a future Cumbre Vieja collapse. They painted a terrifying picture of a huge bulge of water almost a kilometre high swiftly radiating outwards as a series of tsunami in excess of 100m high. Within hours the coastlines of Northwest Africa and Southern Europe would be battered by 50m waves, with South America being struck six hours after collapse. After nine hours, the Caribbean and Eastern Seaboard of the United States would face a barrage by a dozen waves up to 50m high. Without any pre-evacuation, the resulting death toll is predicted to be in the tens of millions.

From ocean bed unrest to coastal choas

An earthquake on the sea bed displaces a huge volume of water but the waves are only 1m or so high and therefore barely detectable in deep water

In shallow water near land the waves slow to 45km/h but by this time they have reached a height of 50m or more. Often, a tsunami compromises several waves and this has often proved lethal to people returning home to salvage their belongings

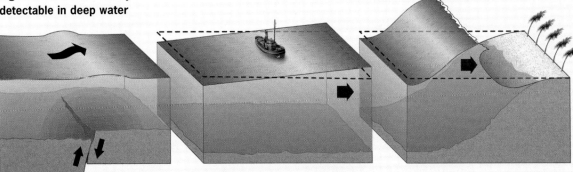

The tsunami speeds towards land at up to 800km/h but it is still able to pass beneath deep sea shipping almost unnoticed because the crests are so low and so far apart

continued

continued

Tsunami factfile

- Tsunamis are rarely alone. More often than not they occur as a series of waves making up a tsunami train. This can come ashore over a period of three or four hours with waves typically spaced from 10 to 60 minutes.
- The most lethal tsunami struck Japan's Awa coast in 1703, taking over 100,000 lives.
- The biggest observed tsunami was caused by a landslide that crashed into Lituya Bay in Alaska in 1958. The 516m (1,720ft) wave sloshed from side to side within the bay, carrying with it two fishing boats whose crew amazingly survived.
- Japan is more affected by tsunamis than any other country. During the last 1,200 years, more than 70 tsunamis have taken well over 100,000 lives.
- Doubling the height of a tsunami will increase the energy fourfold; tripling it increases a tsunami's energy nine times.

From *Focus*

Studying the structure

1 How is the information organised in this text? Think about the text's purpose and audience and in your answer comment on the following:

- layout and design
- use of images
- the different types of information presented.

Looking at language

2 Try to **establish a relationship with the writer**. Scan the text to find three examples of emotive language and comment on how and why the writer has used these. The first example has been selected for you:

- 'Terror in the harbour'

What the writer thinks

3 Close read the text from *'There is no question that tsunamis are killers ...'* to *'... the resulting death toll is predicted to be in the tens of millions.'*

   a What evidence does the writer give to support his claim that *'things may become worse in the future'*?

   b How convincing do you find his claims? **Make judgements** and support your answer with a clear explanation and references to the text.

Text 2

In the 1950s, the mountaineer Herbert Tichy climbed Mount Cho Oyu, the fifth highest mountain in the world. During the climb he experienced a storm of immense proportions – a terrible blizzard with huge winds. Here, Tichy and his three Sherpa guides, Pasang, Adjiba and Ang Nyima, are sheltering in their tent when the storm strikes.

The storm

I felt protected and safe in spite of the utter solitude of our bivouac and although I was perhaps sleeping at a point higher and more remote from the world than any other man alive.

I did not dream that night, but waking was a nightmare and I clung to the hope that it was actually a bad dream. The sound of Pasang groaning convinced me that it was real. The side of the tent was being pressed down on my face by some invisible force, preventing me from breathing, and an uproar of rattling, whistling and screaming filled the air. It took me half a minute to realize what had occurred.

The wind had become a hurricane and had torn our tents from their moorings; the tent pegs had snapped. I put out my hand and felt for Pasang, who was groaning, in his sleep perhaps, or perhaps from a presentiment[1] of disaster to come. Stare as I might, no chink of light was to be seen. It was still night.

By the time daylight glimmered through the canvas, the wind had increased in violence. I can't say whether I had slept in the interval or lain awake, but it was now day and I had to come to some decision. I couldn't lie on in a twilight state between sleeping and waking, between life and death; that would be too easy.

The sun penetrated the yellow fabric. It seemed to promise life and warmth, in strange contrast to the icy hurricane which threatened to hurl us down the mountain-side.

I nudged Pasang again.

"Wait? Go down?" he asked.

continued

[1]presentiment – *sense that something is going to happen*

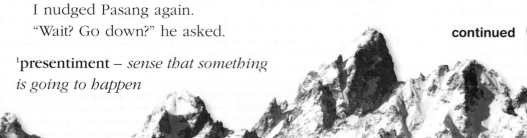

continued ▶

I didn't know which. I didn't even know whether it was morning or evening, whether we had passed a long day in our wretched tents, or whether the sun had just risen and we still had the day to endure.

"We'll see," I added.

We crept out from under the tent. It was not easy, for the wind kept the canvas tight down on us like a fisherman's net and hugged us.

There was not a cloud in the sky. But we could not always see the sky; it was hidden by thick flurries of snow. A hurricane of a force I had never experienced scourged the snow-covered mountainside. The temperature was thirty to thirty-five degrees below zero. The most horrible part of it was the cloudless blue sky.

I crouched down beside Pasang in the snow. We could not stand up. The wind would have thrown us down or lifted us from the ground.

The other tent was also wrecked. The huddled bodies of Ang Nyima and Adjiba were moulded by the flattened canvas. We gave them a prod. They were still alive and crept out to join us. The four of us cowered together beside the flattened tents and stared into the vortex². We could only speak in shouts.

"Never known a storm like this," Pasang shouted. "All die."

He repeated it again and again.

I agreed with him. We should all die.

Adjiba and Ang Nyima said nothing. They sat huddled and dumb, their faces a bluish grey, marked by death – no, dead already. Their dark eyes were fixed on mine, asking no questions, hinting no reproach. They were gates to another world, at whose frontier we had now arrived.

I experienced a strange split in my ego³.

Like Pasang and Adjiba and Ang Nyima, I was a poor wretch, tortured by cold and fear of death, whose only comfort in face of the final and utter solitude⁴ was derived from⁵ the presence of my three companions. And at the same time the other part of me looked down without the least emotion on the four of us. My fate was not at all terrible to this second me. "You've always played fast and loose a bit with this possibility; you can't complain if it has come true. But how can you answer to yourself for the death-stricken faces of these three Sherpas?"

This split personality persisted throughout the events that followed;

²**vortex** – *whirling centre*
³**ego** – *image of oneself*
⁴**solitude** – *death*
⁵**derived from** – *due to*

one part acted instinctively and suffered in the flesh, and the other followed events without feeling or pity, merely as a critical observer, coldly making his own comments upon them.

We were still huddled together, overwhelmed by the violence of nature and incapable of coming to any decision, when suddenly the wind lifted the other tent and threatened to blow it right away. I threw myself on it without thinking and held it down, my body on the tent, my hands in the snow. I had had my mittens stripped off in creeping out of our own tent, but that did not matter very much as I had put my hands in my warm trouser pockets inside an outer windproof smock.

Now they were in contact with the snow, and in the next two or three minutes this is what happened:

The tent was rescued. The Sherpas salvaged it. But I felt a burning sensation in my hands. The pain got worse and throbbed through my whole body.

Probably their warmth melted the snow when they first touched it. The icy hurricane seized on and sucked at the moisture, a hurricane of eighty miles an hour at a temperature of thirty-five degrees below zero.

The pain got worse and worse. I chafed my hands, and beat them against my sides; it did not stop the pain. I thought of creeping into my tent, but it lay like a sail, flat on the snow. I got into a panic, as if I had been on fire – and actually the injuries caused by frost and fire are similar – and started shouting.

The Sherpas, who had been busy so far salvaging the tent, rushed up, and as soon as they realised my disaster, Adjiba hunted under my tent for my mittens.

My watching, critical self showed up again. I saw it all before my eyes as a picture, Pasang and Ang Nyima with their backs pressed against the wind, and myself kneeling crucified between them, my hands outstretched and hidden within the remnants of warmth which might still be my salvation. My animal self relished these few seconds of warmth and shelter.

Adjiba brought my mittens; I seized them. My hands were white and swollen. I felt they were done for, but *we* were not done for yet.

From *Cho Oyu, by favour of the gods* by Herbert Tichy

Studying the structure

1   Scan the text and trace the moments of tension as the storm builds up. For example, the text starts *'I felt protected and safe ...'*, but Herbert Tichy and his team wake up to much more severe weather conditions.

   a   Select appropriate quotations from the text and, in your own words, explain the changes that have occurred in the weather.

   b   Draw an 'emotion graph' of the storm like the one below. On the vertical axis add quotations that show the degrees of intensity of the storm. On the horizontal axis add quotations that show the tension of the mountaineers. **Make a judgement** about which quotations can be linked together to plot your emotion graph.

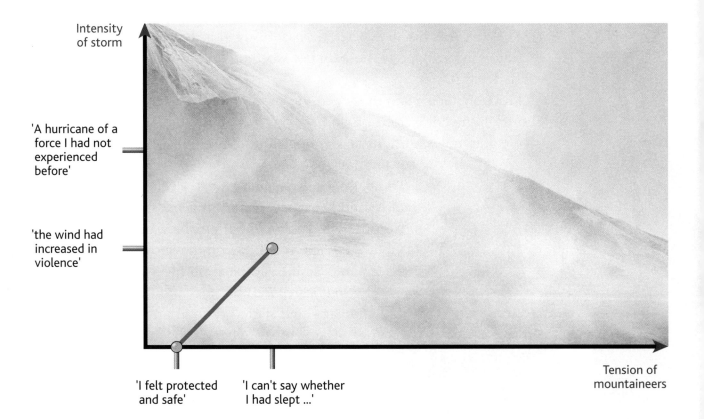

Intensity of storm

'A hurricane of a force I had not experienced before'

'the wind had increased in violence'

'I felt protected and safe'

'I can't say whether I had slept ...'

Tension of mountaineers

2   Close read the section from *'I experienced a strange split in my ego'* to *'My animal self relished these few seconds of warmth and shelter'*. **Rationalise what is happening**. In your own words, explain what the *'strange split'* in Herbert Tichy's ego was.

Born in Jamaica, James Berry is one of the Caribbean's foremost poets. In this poem, he describes a typical hurricane in his native land, where storms of this violent nature are a regular occurrence.

Hurricane

Under low black clouds
the wind was all
speedy feet, all horns and breath,
all bangs, howls, rattles,
in every hen house,
church hall and school.

Roaring, screaming, returning,
it made forced entry, shoved walls,
made rifts, brought roofs down,
hitting rooms to sticks apart.

It wrung soft banana trees,
broke tough trunks of palms.
It pounded vines of yams,
left fields battered up.

Invisible with such ecstasy –
with no intervention of sun or man –
everywhere kept changing branches.

Zinc sheets are kites.
Leaves are panic swarms.
Fowls are fixed with feathers turned.
Goats, dogs, pigs,
all are people together.

Then growling it slunk away
from muddy, mossy trail and boats
in hedges: and cows, ratbats, trees,
fish, all dead in the road.

By James Berry

Looking at language

1 How is the hurricane depicted in this poem?

   a Close read the poem and then comment on the writer's use of figurative language. What is the effect on the reader?

   b Which images in the poem do you find the most effective? Give reasons for your choices.

Studying the structure

2 With a partner, discuss the structure of this poem.

   a What is the focus of each verse?

   b Why do you think the verses are of unequal lengths?

What the writer thinks

3 What is James Berry's attitude towards the hurricane? Find evidence to support your ideas and explain why the writer might have this attitude.

Compare

Which of the three texts do you think conveys the power of our 'Violent Earth' most effectively?

For each text, make notes on the following features.

1 Language

   a What techniques do the different writers use to describe the natural disasters?

   b Compare these techniques and explain which you find the most effective.

2 Structure

   a How does the structure vary between the three texts?

   b How does their structure help the writer to convey the power of the natural disaster?

3 The writer's voice

   a Compare the ways in which the writer's voice speaks to the reader.

   b Which text speaks most directly to you and in what way?

4 Now decide which text conveys the power of our 'Violent Earth' most effectively. Organise your notes carefully and then plan a formal presentation of your views using your notes as prompts. Remember to:

- refer to all three texts when presenting your ideas
- support all your ideas with references to the text and explain and justify them fully.

10 Islands

Introduction

Islands are often popular holiday destinations, holding a fascination for travellers and explorers alike. In this unit, you will look at texts that give information about islands. They each have different purposes, are aimed at different readers and are organised in different ways. To be useful, information has to be clearly explained and easy to find, but it can also entertain through its descriptions, presentation and the point of view of the writer. We are always told that even facts should not be taken at face value and there is plenty of scope for individual readers to interpret these texts differently.

 Cephalonia   Canna   Jamaica

Reading strategies

- relate to previous reading experience
- see images
- infer
- read backward and forwards
- ask questions
- interpret patterns

Pre-reading: infer

1   The following phrases could mean more than one thing. In pairs, work out different meanings that could be **inferred** from each:

   a   a popular resort
   b   five-year-old Jack said it was the best holiday he'd ever had
   c   a picnic site where children can really let off steam.

2   Think of two other phrases of your own that could be interpreted in various ways. Form a group of four and try out your phrases on another pair.

3   Explain why it is possible for us to interpret these phrases differently.

Islands

Text 1

Cephalonia, a Greek island made famous by the book and the film, *Captain Corelli's Mandolin*, is ideal for a relaxing holiday in beautiful surroundings. This text is a website review of the island by a holiday maker who has added comments to the web pages of an online travel company. People searching for holidays would visit the site and see what other people have written about the destination. It aims to persuade you to go and to inform you but it is not a precise brochure description.

CEPHALONIA

> " The half-forgotten island of Cephalonia rises improvidently and inadvisedly from the Ionian sea; it is an island so immense in antiquity that the very rocks themselves exhale nostalgia and the red earth lies stupefied not only by the sun, but by the impossible weight of memory. The ships of Odysseus were built of Cephalonian pine, his bodyguards were Cephalonian giants, and some maintain that his palace was not in Ithaca but in Cephalonia. "

This description of the beautiful Greek island of Cephalonia is taken from the opening pages of Louis de Bernières' best-selling novel, "Captain Corelli's Mandolin". The book is now the subject of a film starring Nicolas Cage, currently being filmed on Cephalonia. Filming is due to finish by the end of August but expect a significant rise in tourist numbers in 2001/02. Beat the rush and go now!

Cephalonia is the largest of the Ionian islands. It's capital, Argóstoli, is a busy town by a bay with a harbour bridge built by the British in the nineteenth century. The town was devastated by the earthquake of 1953 (the single most talked about incident in the island's history) and is full of narrow, bustling streets and shops.

Because of its size, you can't hurry a tour of the island, but driving is rewarding with some stunning scenery, especially along the coasts. Lassi and the resorts of the south-west are popular as is Skala to the south-east. Sami on the east coast is a good base and convenient for hydrofoil trips to other islands including neighbouring Ithaca. It's also the site of the Captain Corelli film set.

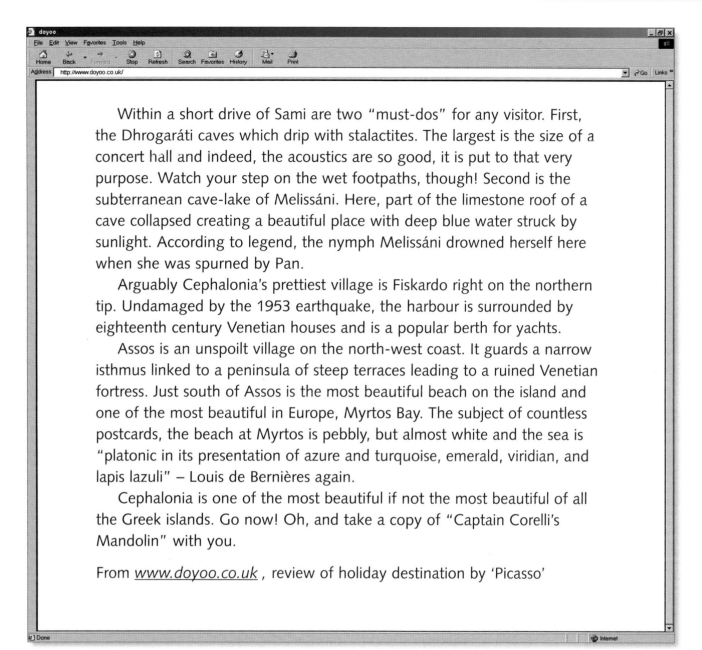

Within a short drive of Sami are two "must-dos" for any visitor. First, the Dhrogaráti caves which drip with stalactites. The largest is the size of a concert hall and indeed, the acoustics are so good, it is put to that very purpose. Watch your step on the wet footpaths, though! Second is the subterranean cave-lake of Melissáni. Here, part of the limestone roof of a cave collapsed creating a beautiful place with deep blue water struck by sunlight. According to legend, the nymph Melissáni drowned herself here when she was spurned by Pan.

Arguably Cephalonia's prettiest village is Fiskardo right on the northern tip. Undamaged by the 1953 earthquake, the harbour is surrounded by eighteenth century Venetian houses and is a popular berth for yachts.

Assos is an unspoilt village on the north-west coast. It guards a narrow isthmus linked to a peninsula of steep terraces leading to a ruined Venetian fortress. Just south of Assos is the most beautiful beach on the island and one of the most beautiful in Europe, Myrtos Bay. The subject of countless postcards, the beach at Myrtos is pebbly, but almost white and the sea is "platonic in its presentation of azure and turquoise, emerald, viridian, and lapis lazuli" – Louis de Bernières again.

Cephalonia is one of the most beautiful if not the most beautiful of all the Greek islands. Go now! Oh, and take a copy of "Captain Corelli's Mandolin" with you.

From *www.doyoo.co.uk* , review of holiday destination by 'Picasso'

Explaining the ideas

1 Close read the text.

    a Visualise the information in the review by drawing a rough map of the island and annotating it with the details given. **Read backwards and forwards** in the text to check you are linking up the places correctly.

    b On your map, highlight the facts, opinions and advice in different colours.

    c What have you learned about the types of information given?

Looking at language

3 The text aims to persuade the reader that Cephalonia is a great island for holidays. How does the language used make it sound interesting?

    a Scan the text to find examples of these different styles of language: formal, poetic, informal, commands. Note down the best example of each.

    b Scan the text and pick out the adjectives used. What meanings can we **infer** from these?

The information about the Scottish island of Canna is taken from a travel book. This type of literature gives a personal account of the writer's travels, so it is more than a guide book or travel brochure. It will include facts about the place and its people but also recount experiences and give the writer's opinions.

canna

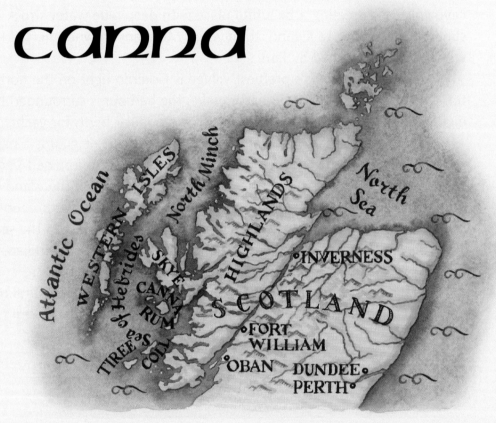

This lovely island has one of the most popular anchorages[1] on the West Coast; spacious and secure in any wind direction thanks to the protective arms of Canna and its connected little-sister island of Sanday. It also has a marvellous climate because the prevailing wind usually whips the clouds straight over to Rum where they hit the mountains and unload their rainy burden.

Having said that, on one of my earliest visits to Canna the rain was coming down so heavily that I almost had to swim through it. I had gone ashore to use the single lonely telephone box (which was painted blue) only to find the old press-button 'A or B' mechanism so jammed with coins that it was unusable and even dialling '100' for the operator drew a blank. I stood in that steamy box, expecting a fish to swim by at any moment and trying to think of a solution when I noticed, scratched among the graffiti, the word 'Try ...' followed by a long number. I tried it, got a dialling tone, and then dialled my required number. Hey presto, I was immediately connected. Long distance, no charge – a Canna miracle!

Canna House, surrounded by thick woodland of native species such as

[1]anchorages – *harbours*

rowan, hazel, ash, oak and birch, interspersed with some Corsican pine and Japanese larch, overlooks the harbour. It was the home of the late Dr John Lorne Campbell and his widow, the American writer Margaret Fay Shaw, who still lives there. Close by is the main farm with fields of delicious early potatoes or good old-fashioned haystacks creating a rural scene of yesteryear. A large herd of pedigree Highland cattle crop the fallow land and Cheviot sheep roam the hills.

In 1881 the island was bought by Robert Thom, a Glasgow shipowner, for £23,000. He was a benevolent landlord and in 1938 his family looked for a worthy successor. They chose the Gaelic scholar, farmer and 'bonny fechter', John Lorne Campbell. Campbell worked for most of his life on the preservation of Gaelic culture and he and his wife assembled the world's biggest library of Celtic literature and music. When in 1981 he, in turn, looked for a suitable guardian he chose to hand over Canna with its small community of about twenty islanders, and its priceless library, to the National Trust for Scotland.

It is worthwhile spending some time exploring this fascinating island because there is so much to see. A road runs west from the harbour beneath a basalt escarpment to Tarbert Bay where there is both a ruined fort and the remains of an ancient nunnery dating from the time when Canna belonged to Iona. On the north side of this central neck a well-preserved Viking ship burial was discovered and signs of Viking occupation are clearly visible. A rectangular outline of boulders is known as the grave of the King of Norway (Uaigh Righ Lochlainn).

Beyond Tarbert Bay the walk westwards to Garrisdale Point, with its two Iron Age forts and fortified wall, is more challenging as the track virtually disappears, but many of the most interesting features are quite close to the harbour and one of these is rarely seen by visitors. Through the gate, up the short hill-road beside the main farmhouse, and concealed by a hillock beyond the cemetery is the site of the original 19th-century 'township' with a broken Celtic cross of exquisite workmanship, remnants of an early 7th-century chapel, and, on a nearby hummock a standing stone with a small hole in it at head height. This is called a pillory stone because, so we are told, an offender's thumb could be jammed in it!

The islanders are Catholic and worship in a modest building by the farmhouse. The ornate Catholic church standing on Sanday, the most conspicuous landmark on approaching the harbour, was built by Lady Bute in memory of her father but fell into serious disrepair. Happily, it is now being converted into a Gaelic Study Centre with accommodation for eighteen guests.

East of the harbour, near the ferry pier, is a charming little Protestant church, constructed in 1914 as a memorial to Robert Thom, with a conical bell tower and vaulted roof like early Celtic churches. Behind it is an unusual rocky pinnacle with a medieval prison tower on top where a Clanranald chief imprisoned his wife to keep her from her lover – a MacLeod from Skye.

From *An Island Odyssey* by Hamish Haswell Smith

Studying the structure and looking at language

1 Continuously read the whole extract to become familiar with the content, structure and language.

2 In a group of four, close read the text to investigate one feature of the text. Make sure that each member of the group investigates a different feature of the text. Use the prompts in the table below as a starting point.

Feature of the text	Notes and examples from the text.
Purpose • Why the text was written. • Who the text was written for. • How will it be used?	
Structure and organisation • How the whole text is structured. • How links are made between paragraphs. • How links are made within paragraphs.	
Sentences • Viewpoint (first person, third person, etc ...). • Main tenses used. • Length and structure of the sentences. • How punctuation contributes to meaning.	
Vocabulary • Words and phrases used (formal, informal) • How much description is used? • What effects are created by the choice of words?	

As you read, it will help if you **relate the text to previous reading experience** and **ask questions** about why the writer has written the text in this way.

3 Report back to the group on the feature you have investigated. Then make notes on the features of the text that other members of your group have investigated.

Islands

This text is an entry in an encyclopedia about different countries and the people who live there. Information is given to the reader in a variety of ways, which adds to their interest. Information texts, compared with other texts, are often read differently. Readers are looking for particular information so search for it rather than read the text in full from top to bottom. What other texts do you know where this happens?

JAMAICA

PATOIS

Many Jamaicans speak a dialect called Patois. It is basically English, but also includes Portuguese, West African and Spanish words.

▼ *The Dunn's River Falls are a major attraction on the island, which is crossed by many free-flowing streams and rivers. Even the name Jamaica comes from a Native American word meaning 'island of springs'.*

Christopher Columbus described Jamaica as "the fairest island that eyes have beheld". Sandy beaches lined with palm trees lead to fertile, low-lying coastal plains. Mountains, with cooler temperatures, cover most of the island and the northwest has limestone highlands. The only things that spoil this image of paradise are the hurricanes which can cause terrible damage.

Spain conquered this island in 1494. The Spanish treated the native Arawak people so badly that most of them died. In the 1600s the British arrived, seized control and turned Jamaica into a huge slave market. Slavery was abolished in 1838, but friction grew between workers and plantation owners. British troops stopped a revolt in 1865 and Jamaica was made a British crown colony. By the 1940s the island had won some independence and it became fully independent in 1962. Since then Jamaica has set up its own parliament and everyone over the age of 18 can vote.

Most Jamaicans are descendants of African slaves brought to the island by the Spanish and the British. Others are descended from white Europeans, Asians or Middle Eastern traders. Nearly two thirds of the islanders now live in cities, often in overcrowded slums. The economy relies heavily on agriculture and mining. Tourism is also important. Every year over 850,000 tourists visit Jamaica, attracted by the warm climate and beautiful scenery.

continued ▶

continued ▼

▲ *Fashionable Montego Bay is a popular stopping-off point for cruise ships.*

▲ *Rastafarians are Jamaicans who look to Africa as their homeland. Many wear their hair in long dreadlocks.*

▲ *Cricket is a popular sport in Jamaica. It is played and watched by young and old alike. The game was originally brought to Jamaica by the British. Nowadays Jamaicans regularly play for the West Indies cricket team.*

FACTS AND FIGURES

Area: 11,430 sq km

Population: 2,495,000

Capital: Kingston (588,000)

Other major city: Spanish Town (93,000)

Highest point: Blue Mt Peak (2,256 m)

Official language: English

Main religion: Christianity

Currency: Jamaican dollar

Main exports: Sugar, bauxite, alumina, bananas, fruit

Government: Constitutional monarchy

Per capita GNP: US $1,340

From *Kingfisher Encyclopedia of Lands and Peoples* by Larousse

Explaining the ideas

1 Spend five minutes close reading the encyclopedia entry about Jamaica. Try to take in as much information about the island as you can.

   a In pairs, take it in turns to **ask a question** about Jamaica for your partner to answer. Did you both remember similar things about the island or different information?

   b Look at the list of reading strategies on pages 7 and 8. Make a note of the strategies you think you used when you were reading the entry. Are there any others that you could have used?

Studying the structure

2 **a** Make a list of the different ways of presenting information that are used on these pages. Explain why each of these is an appropriate way of giving that piece of information.

   b Close read the main text section. Identify which information is also referred to elsewhere on the page and which information is mentioned only in the main text section.

▶ Compare

Text 1: Cephalonia and Text 2: Canna both inform and describe islands for potential travellers. Compare the structure of each text by creating a flow chart for each.

1 Working in pairs, take one text each. On a large piece of paper draw a flow chart down the page, with one box to represent each paragraph. Make the boxes big enough to write about 10–15 words in and leave room in between each box for an arrow and additional notes.

2 Skim read the text, **reading backwards and forwards,** and make notes in each box explaining the main content of the paragraph.

3 Where you notice a clear link being made by the writer between one paragraph and the next, note down the quotation or explain the link beside the arrow.

The first two boxes for Text 2: Canna have been done for you. This is what your chart should look like:

> Two positive features explained quite fully: sheltered harbour and good weather.

'Having said that' makes a contrast with the weather conditions mentioned in first paragraph.

> • Describes previous visit.
> • Contrast in weather: torrential rain.
> • Humorous mention of a lucky incident.

4 When you have finished your text, place your flow chart beside your partner's and compare them. **Interpret the patterns** to work out the similarities and differences in the structure of the two texts. Annotate the sheet with your observations in a different colour.

5 For the really adventurous, try comparing these flow charts with one for Text 3: Jamaica. Remember that the main text makes references to draw in the other bits of information presented on the page. How could you present it as a flow chart? What are the similarities and differences in the structure?

11 Aliens and UFOs

Introduction

Since the first landing on the Moon in 1968 we have become increasingly preoccupied with the search for other life forms. Many books, films and television shows deal with life on other planets as if it really exists. In this unit you are going to read three texts which look at this topic from different angles. The big question for us all is: 'Is there anybody out there?'

 Text 1 The War of the Worlds

 Text 2 Explore the universe/ Age of Mythology

 Text 3 Alien contact

Reading strategies

- infer
- deduce
- speculate
- establish a relationship with the narrator

Pre-reading: speculate

1 Do you believe that there might be life on another planet? Do you believe in UFOs and aliens? Discuss your ideas with a partner, giving reasons for your opinions.

2 What do you think would happen if aliens did land on Earth? How do you think people would react? Share your ideas with a partner and then feedback your ideas in a whole class discussion.

3 Were you surprised by any of your classmates' ideas about aliens and UFOs?

Text 1 Aliens and UFOs

This is an extract from a science fiction novel, *The War of the Worlds* by the author H. G. Wells. Here, a UFO from Mars has just landed on Earth. A crowd has gathered to witness the gradual emergence of a Martian from the cylinder-shaped spacecraft. The narrator describes the scene.

I think everyone expected to see a man emerge – possibly something a little unlike us terrestrial men, but in all essentials a man. I know I did. But, looking, I presently saw something stirring within the shadow – greyish billowy movements, one above another, and then two luminous discs like eyes. Then something resembling a little grey snake, about the thickness of a walking-stick, coiled up out of the writhing middle, and wriggled in the air towards me – and then another.

A sudden chill came over me. There was a loud shriek from a woman behind. I half turned, keeping my eyes fixed upon the cylinder still, from which other tentacles were now projecting, and began pushing my way back from the edge of the pit. I saw astonishment giving place to horror on the faces of the people about me. I heard inarticulate[1] exclamations on all sides. There was a general movement backward. I saw the shopman struggling still on the edge of the pit. I found myself alone, and saw the people on the other side of the pit running off. I looked again at the cylinder, and ungovernable terror gripped me. I stood petrified and staring.

A big greyish, rounded bulk, the size perhaps, of a bear, was rising slowly and painfully out of the cylinder. As it bulged up and caught the light, it glistened like wet leather. Two large dark-coloured eyes were regarding me steadfastly. It was rounded, and had, one might say, a face. There was a mouth under the eyes, the lipless brim of which quivered and panted, and dropped saliva. The body heaved and pulsated convulsively. A lank tentacular appendage gripped the edge of the cylinder, another swayed in the air.

Those who have never seen a living Martian can scarcely imagine the strange horror of their appearance. The peculiar V-shaped mouth with its pointed upper lip, the absence of brow ridges, the absence of a chin beneath the wedge-like lower lip, the incessant quivering of this mouth, the Gorgon groups of tentacles, the tumultuous breathing of the lungs in a strange atmosphere, the evident heaviness and painfulness of movement, due to the greater gravitational energy of the earth – above all, the extraordinary intensity of the immense eyes – culminated in an effect akin to nausea. There was something fungoid in the oily brown skin, something in the clumsy deliberation of their tedious movements unspeakably terrible. Even at this first encounter, this first glimpse, I was overcome with disgust and dread.

From *The War of the Worlds* by HG Wells

[1]inarticulate – *unclear*

Looking at language

1 Read the first paragraph closely. **Establish a relationship with the narrator**. How is a sense of the narrator's increasing fear built up? You should comment on:

- what the narrator sees
- the narrator's description of his feelings.
- what the narrator hears

Interpreting the meanings

2 Close read the rest of the text. Working in pairs, pick out any words that convey the *'strange horror'* of the alien. Consider both the appearance of the alien and the way it moves. When you have picked out the words comment on what you **infer** from:

- any powerful adjectives you have selected
- the adverbs you have chosen
- the use of sentence structure to add emphasis to particular words.

Reasons for writing

3 This text is written in the first person. What is the effect of this on the reader? Support your answer with examples from the text.

2 Aliens and UFOs

The following two advertisements were printed in a magazine called *Focus*. Both advertisements present contrasting perspectives on the idea of life beyond Earth.

Explore the Universe
from Jodrell Bank

A programme of part-time courses in astronomy

Life in the Universe and SETI
An introduction to astronomy which focuses on our own cosmic origins and discusses progress in the search for extraterrestrial life.

Introduction to Radio Astronomy
A short course featuring the opportunity to use our radio telescopes either in a weekend visit to Jodrell Bank or over the internet.

Explore the Radio Universe
Our major course on radio astronomy describing its history, techniques and achievements. Students will make their own observations and analyse data from the Jodrell Bank telescopes.

Frontiers of Modern Astronomy
A more advanced course explaining Jodrell research on Stellar Explosions, Pulsars, Gravitational Lenses, the Big Bang and the Cosmic Microwave Background.

Courses consist of 12–24 weeks of part-time home study and lead to the award of Certificates of Credit which can count towards higher awards. Fees range from £115–£165 for UK/EU students.

Further details and instructions on how to apply are available on our website.
Astronomy Distance Learning, Jodrell Bank Observatory, The University of Manchester, Macclesfield, Cheshire SK11 9DL, United Kingdom.
E-mail: DL-INFO@jb.man.ac.uk Tel: 01477 572650 Fax: 01477 571618
www.jb.man.ac.uk/distance

From The University of Manchester

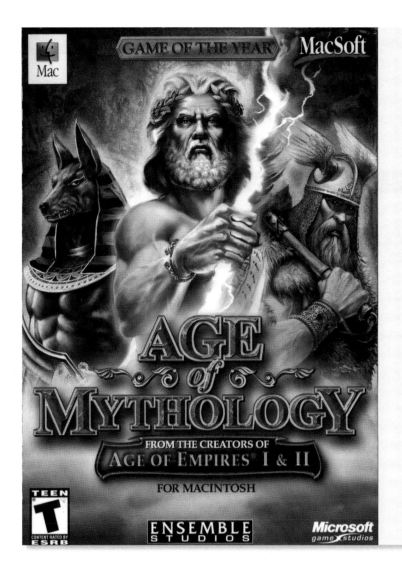

Interpreting the meanings

1 Skim read the advertisements to get a general idea of what they are about. Both advertisements were included in a magazine called *Focus*. In pairs **speculate** about:

- what type of magazine this might be
- who would read this magazine.

Support your answer with evidence from the texts.

Looking at language and studying the structure

2 Both adverts offer the possibility of a life beyond Earth experience but in very different ways. Compare and contrast how they do this. Use a table like the one below to help you record your ideas:

Feature	Explore the universe	Age of Mythology
Headings		
Layout and organisation of ideas		
Language		
Images		

Aliens and UFOs

Some people claim to have had close encounters with UFOs and a few even say that they have been abducted by aliens. This information text recounts the 'real life' experience of Betty and Barney who claimed to have been kidnapped by aliens whilst driving back from a holiday in Canada in 1961.

Alien contact

Shortly after they drove past the village of Lancaster, Betty noticed two bright lights near the Moon. One seemed to be getting larger. She pointed them out to Barney, who thought they might be a satellite that had gone off course.

The larger light stayed with them for several miles, appearing and disappearing behind mountains and treetops. By now they were beginning to feel a little worried. The thing, whatever it was, seemed to be circling round them and there were no other cars on the road.

Betty took out the binoculars again. By now the UFO was close enough for her to see that it was some sort of enormous aircraft with a double row of windows. Barney stopped the car again, in the middle of the road this time, took the binoculars from Betty and got out.

Barney started to walk towards the object, which dropped down to hover about treetop height. When he was about fifty metres away and still using the binoculars, he was able to see about a dozen people staring down at him from the mystery craft.

The UFO dropped in altitude and seemed to lower down some sort of ladder or ramp. Then one of the occupants emerged. Barney continued to watch the creatures in the craft. To his horror he found he was having difficulty looking away from their eyes, which seemed to exert a curious, almost hypnotic, influence over him. Gripped by sudden panic, Barney screamed and ran back to the car. He drove off shouting that he was sure they were 'going to be captured'. But in fact nothing happened. Or almost nothing.

Neither Barney nor Betty could see the strange craft now, not even as a distant light. They heard a beeping sound and felt momentarily sleepy. Then came some further beeping sounds. The road seemed unfamiliar but when they saw a sign to Concord they realized where they were and drove directly home.

Oddly enough, they arrived home in daylight. Both their watches had stopped, but clocks in the house showed it was now 5 a.m., two to two and a half hours later than Barney had originally anticipated. During the journey, Betty had asked Barney, 'Now do you believe in UFOs?' But despite his fright, Barney told her he did not.

The Hills went to bed and slept exhausted until three that afternoon. When they woke, their experience the night before seemed unreal. But Betty examined their car and found several shiny circles, each about the size of a large coin, burned into the paintwork of the boot. A compass brought close to them spun wildly. It looked as if something very real had happened to them.

Much against Barney's better judgement, Betty reported their sighting to the local Air Force Base where details were logged. Within days she had started to have nightmares of being seized and carried off in a UFO.

The investigation

A month after the Hills had their frightening experience, the National Investigations Committee on Aerial Phenomena (NICAP) became involved. This Washington-based organization avoided crank reports like the plague, but occasionally investigated the more serious and puzzling UFO sightings.

NICAP experts interviewed the Hills and were impressed. As word spread, other experts became involved. Betty was still having nightmares. Barney remained uncomfortable discussing his experience. Two suggestions were made to them. The first was that they should retrace the steps of their interrupted journey. The second was that hypnosis might help them recall more clearly what had happened.

The Hills took up the first suggestion and while their return trip to Route 3 triggered no further memories, they did discover something very interesting. When they called at a small restaurant near the town of Woodstock, local residents told them of several UFO sightings in the area. The descriptions of these UFOs – one of which hovered for almost an hour – sounded suspiciously like the craft they had seen.

It was not until February of 1964 that the Hills took up the second suggestion.

The story

Dr Simon regressed[1] both Betty and Barney Hill in a series of sessions over a period of six months. The stories they told matched, but what they remembered under hypnosis was almost unbelievable. The reconstruction of the events of 19 September was roughly as follows:

Sometime after they saw the UFO, a group of between 8 and 11 small, grey men (or at least humanoids) with strange eyes, in matching uniforms and military-style caps stepped into the road and stopped their car. The leader – whom Barney thought was evil – told them they would not be harmed.

Despite this reassurance, they were both taken on board a disc-shaped aircraft where they were physically examined. Samples of hair, fingernails and

---

[1]**regressed** – *hypnotic regression is a technique where hypnotised patients are taken back in time to remember things*

continued ▶

continued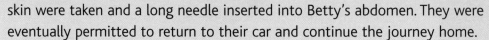

skin were taken and a long needle inserted into Betty's abdomen. They were eventually permitted to return to their car and continue the journey home.

During the two hours they were aboard the strange craft Betty asked the leader where he came from. He showed her a map of a distant star system.

The diagnosis

Many people found the Hill's story hard to believe. On the face of it, this seemed to be yet another 'encounter' with Flash Gordon-style aliens who claimed to come from the depths of the galaxy yet looked human, wore no spacesuits and had little difficulty breathing the terrestrial air. Dr Simon concluded their accounts were fantasy. And there the case might have rested, but for one worrying detail.

The star map

After one of her sessions with Dr Simon, Betty drew the star map she claimed the leader had shown her. There was nothing in the night sky that looked remotely like it and, like the rest of her story, it was dismissed as fiction.

But years after the event, in 1974, Dr Walter Mitchell, an astronomer at Ohio State University, collaborated with Marjory Fish to take a fresh look at the evidence.

Ms Fish argued that if the map were genuine, it would be drawn from the viewpoint of the aliens' own solar system. Using a computer programme, Ms Fish and Dr Mitchell discovered that the map showed the night sky as seen not from Earth, but from the distant star Zeta Reticuli.

More puzzling details were to follow. Betty Hill accurately drew Zeta Reticuli as a *double* star, but this fact was not known, even to professional astronomers, in 1964.

From *Alien Contact* by Herbie Brennan

Interpreting the meanings

1 Both Barney and Betty had the same experience but their reactions to it were very different. Describe their reactions and give possible reasons for their different attitudes. You should comment on:
   - their reactions on sighting the UFO
   - their reactions immediately after the event
   - their reactions during and after the investigation.

2 Is there any evidence in this text to support Betty's assertion that she was abducted? What evidence is there that Betty and Barney's accounts might be fantasy? Find evidence in the text to support either point of view.

3 **Speculate.** What do you think about Betty and Barney's account of their 'extraterrestrial' experience? Discuss your point of view with a partner.

Compare

Each of the texts that you have read makes reference to the possibility of extraterrestrial life. Compare the description of the arrival of the Martian in Text 1 with the description in Text 3 of Betty and Barney's encounter with the aliens.

1 Work in a group of four. Firstly, split into two pairs. Each pair should look at one text and discuss how it tries to persuade the reader that aliens might exist. Copy out and complete the table below:

	Text 1: The War of the Worlds	Text 3: Alien contact
Purpose • What text type is it? • Why has it been written? • What is the intended effect on the reader?		
Viewpoint • What voices are used: first, second or third person? • What is the effect?		
Language • Is it factual, scientific, emotive? • Do the writers use powerful adjectives? • Comment on the verbs and adverbs used. • What variety of sentence structures is there in both texts?		

2 Reassemble in your group of four. Discuss how each text tries to persuade the reader that aliens exist. Then discuss what differences and what similarities you have found between the two texts.

3 Which of the texts that you read had the greatest appeal to you? Give reasons for your choice and support your ideas with reference to the text.

12 Food, glorious food

Introduction

Food plays an important role in all our lives. In the past, some foods such as chocolate were seen as luxury goods and enjoyed only by the privileged few, while the poor had to struggle to find enough to eat. Nowadays, a wide variety of food from all over the world is readily available in supermarkets, but concerns about its quality and effects on our health still remain.

 Text 1 The story of Cadbury's chocolate

 Text 2 Food has four seasons

 Text 3 Oliver Twist

Reading strategies

- relate to your own experience
- read backwards and forwards
- infer
- relate to previous reading experience
- establish a relationship with the writer
- deduce

Pre-reading: relate to your own experience

1 Food serves many purposes in our lives. It can be the source of great pleasure (going out for a delicious meal), but the lack of it can be a cause of great distress (the victims of famine). Working with a partner, write down words and phrases that can be associated with the word 'food'.

2 Then organise your ideas into two bullet point lists showing the negative and positive aspects of food.

3 Share your ideas with the rest of the group. Look at the words that you have collected as a group. Do you have more positive or more negative words? What do the number of positive and negative words and the types of words you have collated suggest about your class's attitudes towards food?

Food, glorious food

If we have a craving for chocolate we only need to go to our nearest newsagent or supermarket and we are faced with an overwhelming selection to choose from. But this has not always been the case. This information text about the story of Cadbury's chocolate explores how chocolate has evolved from being a luxury item to something that is readily available to us.

THE STORY OF
Cadbury's
CHOCOLATE

The origins of chocolate can be traced back to the Aztec and Mayan civilisations in Central America. Reputedly, Christopher Columbus introduced the cocoa bean to Europe, but in fact it was his fellow explorer, the Spanish Conquistador Don Cortez, who first realised its commercial value.

When Don Cortez discovered Mexico City, capital of the Aztecs, in 1519, he is said to have been introduced to the spicy drink known as *chocolatl* by Emperor Montezuma himself. This thick, rich drink, made from ground cocoa beans, mixed with maize meal and flavoured with vanilla and chilli, had been consumed in the area for hundreds of years.

When Cortez brought the cocoa beans back to Spain, the flavour of the drink was improved by heating it and adding sugar. The way in which it was prepared was kept a closely guarded secret for almost a century.

The custom of drinking chocolate eventually spread to England in the mid-seventeenth century, but it was a very expensive luxury. When the first 'Chocolate Houses' opened in London in 1657, chocolate cost the equivalent of 50–75 pence a pound, when the pound sterling was worth considerably more than it is today. The Chocolate Houses sold chocolate as a drink and also a pressed cake from which the drink could be made in the home. Chocolate remained a luxury until 1853, when Gladstone's government reduced the very heavy import duty.

～～～～～ THE ONE-MAN BUSINESS ～～～～～

93 Bull Street, a one-man grocery business opened in 1824 in a fashionable shopping area of Birmingham, was the foundation of Cadbury Ltd; today Cadbury are one of the world's largest producers of chocolate. The young Quaker[1], John Cadbury, was twenty-two years old when he opened his shop to sell not only tea but coffee, hops, mustard and two new side-lines – cocoa and drinking chocolate – which he prepared himself using a mortar and pestle.

By 1831 he had become a manufacturer of cocoa and drinking chocolate, with a warehouse in Crooked Lane, Birmingham. The earliest preserved price list of 1842 shows that John Cadbury sold sixteen lines of drinking chocolate in cake and powder with names such as Churchman's Chocolate and Fine Brown Chocolate, plus eleven lines of cocoa including Granulated Cocoa and Homeopathic Cocoa, in addition to French eating chocolate.

1853 saw the first Royal Warrant being awarded as manufacturers of cocoa and chocolate to Queen Victoria, and the company has held Royal Warrants of Appointment ever since. In 1861, John Cadbury retired, handing over the business to his sons, Richard and George. These two Cadbury brothers, particularly George, were the cornerstones of this family business which was to grow into an internationally renowned company.

From *Cadbury's the Taste of Chocolate* by Patricia Dunbar

[1]**Quaker** – *a member of the religious society*

Explaining the ideas

1 Skim read the text quickly to get an idea of what it is about. Then scan the text, identifying the important events in the history of chocolate. Present this information as a timeline or flow chart.

Studying the structure

2 Close read the text. **Relate to your previous reading experience**. How is this text typical of an information text? **Read backwards and forwards** and comment on the following features:

a Layout of information:

- sequencing of information
- visual conventions.

b Language conventions:

- voice
- vocabulary
- connectives
- tense
- length of sentence
- cohesion.

Text 2

Food, glorious food

The writer of this article from the broadsheet newspaper, *The Guardian*, argues that British consumers place more importance on the cost of food than on its quality. The writer believes that the quality of food should concern us more than the cost.

Food has four seasons

Britain is the cheap food capital of the world. That is not the same as saying that the food in Britain is actually cheap. In fact, it is possibly the most expensive in Europe, but we devote less of our disposable income to buying it than any other European country. Price is the fundamental criterion[1] by which food is judged. "It only cost £1.99," we say. "It's dirt cheap." "A snip at ...' Never mind the quality, feel the weight.

It seems pertinent to ask some fundamental questions about the whole concept of 'cheap food': what effects cheap food policies have had on those who produce it and those who choose to eat it, and who, at the end of the day, is responsible for it.

If price becomes the defining criterion for selling food, then it must become the defining criterion for producing it as well. There is enormous pressure on supermarket buyers to find the cheapest source. Food is cheap to produce either because labour and land are cheap, or because the farming process has become so highly industrialised – which is not necessarily the same as efficient – that production is intensified, and labour has largely ceased to exist.

As a consequence, much of our food comes from countries where food is so cheap to produce that even with the cost of bringing it here, it is still cheaper than producing it here. So we import over £18bn of foodstuffs, £10bn more than we export. And as a result of enthusiastically embracing industrial agricultural practices ourselves, we have BSE, endemic listeria, salmonella and E-coli poisoning, and levels of pesticides which have led, for example, to the government until quite recently recommending cutting off the top and bottom 2cm of carrots and peeling them before cooking.

And, as a further consequence of our enthusiastic endorsement of 'cheap food' policies, 50% of men and 33% of women are overweight, with 21% of men and 25% of women officially obese. Diet related diseases – cancer and heart disease, in particular – are the biggest drain on NHS resources, not to mention the biggest killer in the country.

[1]criterion – *quality*

Does this worry us? Apparently not. The vast majority of the population neither know nor care very much about how or why their food is produced, so long as it is 'cheap'.

Britain ceased being an agrarian[2] society 50 or so years ago, but in the last 20 years, we have become utterly urban in thought and word, as well as fact. Only urban criteria define the policies and principles of food production – is it fashionable? is it healthy? is it cheap? And we have delegated the responsibilities for its quality control to any agency other than ourselves, to the government, to the Food Standards Agency, to the environmental health officers, to supermarkets, to journalists for heaven's sake.

And if we do not know how our food is produced, how can we care? We no longer trust our own judgement because we can no longer be bothered to make one. We have come to regard the countryside as a local amenity and the farmers, in that ridiculous phrase, as 'custodians of the countryside'. Keep it coming and keep it 'cheap', those are the governing criteria for food production today.

By Matthew Fort from *The Guardian*

[2]agrarian – *farming*

Studying the structure

1 Close read the text. How are the ideas developed in this text?

  a Now scan each paragraph, selecting key words and phrases. Summarise in a sentence or phrase the key point being made in each paragraph.

  b How is the information sequenced in this text? **Read backwards and forwards** to clarify your understanding and make links.

Looking at language

2 What techniques does the writer use to persuade us that *'Britain is the cheap food capital of the world'*? Copy and complete the table below by picking out rhetorical devices from the text and commenting on their effect.

Point (rhetorical device)	Evidence (example from the text)	Explanation (effect on reader)
Rhetorical questions		
Opinion presented as fact		
Irony		
Repetition		
Tone		
Emotive language		
Figurative language		
Inclusive pronouns		

Food, glorious food

Charles Dickens wrote *Oliver Twist* in 1837. The novel, set in early nineteenth century London, follows the life of an orphaned boy, Oliver. In this extract, Dickens describes the poor conditions and cruelty experienced by Oliver and the other boys living in the orphanage.

Oliver Twist

The room in which the boys were fed, was a large stone hall, with a copper at one end: out of which the master, dressed in an apron for the purpose, and assisted by one or two women, ladled the gruel at meal-times. Of this festive composition each boy had one porringer, and no more – except on occasions of great public rejoicing, when he had two ounces and a quarter of bread besides. The bowls never wanted washing. The boys polished them with their spoons till they shone again; and when they had performed this operation (which never took very long, the spoons being nearly as large as the bowls), they would sit staring at the copper, with such eager eyes, as if they could have devoured the very bricks of which it was composed; employing themselves, meanwhile, in sucking their fingers most assiduously, with the view of catching up any stray splashes of gruel that might have been cast thereon. Boys have generally excellent appetites. Oliver Twist and his companions suffered the tortures of slow starvation for three months: at last they got so voracious and wild with hunger, that one boy, who was tall for his age, and hadn't been used to that sort of thing (for his father had kept a small cookshop), hinted darkly to his companions, that unless he had another basin of gruel *per diem,* he was afraid he might some night happen to eat the boy who slept next him, who happened to be a weakly youth of tender age. He had a wild, hungry eye; and they implicitly believed him. A council was held; lots were cast who should walk up to the master after supper that evening, and ask for more; and it fell to Oliver Twist.

The evening arrived; the boys took their places. The master, in his cook's uniform, stationed himself at the copper; his pauper assistants ranged themselves behind him; the gruel was served out; and a long grace was said over the short commons. The gruel disappeared; the boys whispered each other, and winked at Oliver; while his next neighbours nudged him. Child as he was, he was desperate with hunger, and reckless with misery. He rose from the table; and advancing to the master, basin and spoon in hand, said: somewhat alarmed at his own temerity:

'Please, sir, I want some more.'

The master was a fat, healthy man; but he turned very pale. He gazed in stupefied astonishment on the small rebel for some seconds, and then clung for support to the copper. The assistants were paralysed with wonder; the boys with fear.

'What!' said the master at length, in a faint voice.

'Please, sir,' replied Oliver, 'I want some more.'

The master aimed a blow at Oliver's head with the ladle; pinioned him in his arms; and shrieked aloud for the beadle.

The board were sitting in solemn conclave, when Mr. Bumble rushed into the room in great excitement, and addressing the gentleman in the high chair, said,

'Mr. Limbkins, I beg your pardon, sir! Oliver Twist has asked for more!'

There was a general start. Horror was depicted on every countenance.

'For *more!*' said Mr. Limbkins. 'Compose yourself, Bumble, and answer me distinctly. Do I understand that he asked for more, after he had eaten the supper allotted by the dietary?'

'He did, sir,' replied Bumble.

'That boy will be hung,' said the gentleman in the white waistcoat. 'I know that boy will be hung.'

Oliver was ordered into instant confinement; and a bill was next morning pasted on the outside of the gate, offering a reward of five pounds to anybody who would take Oliver Twist off the hands of the parish.

From *Oliver Twist* by Charles Dickens

Interpreting the meanings

1 Close read the text. How do we know that Dickens' sympathy lies with the children? **Read backwards and forwards** finding examples from the text. Remember you will need to **infer**. You should look at:

- the way in which Oliver and the other children are described (eg *'sucking their fingers most assiduously'* which suggests just how hungry the boys were)

- the way that the adults are portrayed (eg contrast their physical description with the condition of the boys)

- the physical environment of the school (eg the dining room is described as '*a large stone hall*' which suggests an inhospitable and cold environment).

Record your ideas on a table like the one below:

Point	Evidence	Explanation
Dickens highlights the lack of food	He describes the boys as 'sucking their fingers most assiduously'.	This suggests that the boys are so desperately hungry that they are making sure that they have eaten every last bit of the gruel.

The text in its time and place

2 Dickens wrote to entertain his public but also to highlight social concerns. What comment on the society he lived in do you think that Dickens is making in this text?

Compare

In the early nineteenth century when Cadbury Ltd was being established in Birmingham, Dickens described the poverty and starvation facing orphans in another city, London. You are going to compare Text 1: The story of Cadbury's chocolate with Text 3: Oliver Twist.

Imagine that you are a journalist in the nineteenth century. You have been sent to report on the story of Cadbury Ltd in Birmingham. You have also been given another assignment in London to visit and report on the conditions of orphans in the city.

1   Prepare two short oral reports on each of these subjects for audiences of this time. You should consider the following points when compiling your reports:

   a   the different roles of food in each text (luxury item or essential)

   b   the presentation of the theme of food (is it shown in a positive light or does it have negative consequences?)

   c   the tone of each report (upbeat and positive or more serious?)

   d   the content of each report (select information that would appeal to the audience's interest and provide some relevant background information).

2   Once you have scripted your reports, join with a partner and present your reports to each other. You could tape record your reports and present them to the class.

Introduction

From an early age we grow and develop through exploring the world around us. Those first tentative but exciting discoveries often stay with us into adulthood and for some can lead to a desire for exploration beyond our everyday lives. This thirst for knowledge and adventure has produced some of our most famous explorers and taken us into new worlds. The texts in this unit investigate the theme of exploration, both on our planet and beyond.

 Text 1 In search of the true explorer

 Text 2 Up the Amazon

 Text 3 Jim, our scans now show ...

Reading strategies

- see images
- interpret patterns
- read backwards and forwards
- rationalise what is happening
- infer

Pre-reading: rationalise what is happening

1 Why do people explore? In pairs discuss the theme of exploration. You may want to consider the following ideas:

- changes in exploration over time
- the dangers and risks facing explorers
- different kinds of explorer from the past and today.

2 From your discussions produce a list of the characteristics and qualities which you think all explorers have, under the heading: 'Profile of an explorer'.

New worlds

This text, written in 2002, is an article from the magazine, *Geographical*. In this extract, the writer considers the history of exploration and seeks to define what it means to be an explorer today.

In search of the true EXPLORER

Think of an explorer and the image that typically springs to mind depicts a man in a pith helmet sweating his way through the undergrowth, a troupe of overburdened porters trailing behind him. He's most likely wearing khaki, probably in the tropics and almost definitely Victorian. He's certainly a man and always white.

This caricature, which is gradually evolving into someone resembling Indiana Jones has been branded on our subconscious. It's a powerful, defining image, but as a portrayal of someone at the forefront of discovery, it is clearly incorrect.

For a start, it suggests that the process of discovery peaked long ago, with Livingstone and Stanley perhaps. But the truth is, when it comes to exploration, we're still literally skimming the surface. Caver Andrew Eavis, for example, has discovered not only more physical terrain than anyone alive, but also more of what was genuinely unknown than most of the great trailblazers of yesteryear.

And according to astronaut Edwin 'Buzz' Aldrin, we still have better maps of the surface of the moon than of the sea floor. The sea is the world's largest habitat, "home to the least-understood members of the web of life," says deep-sea zoologist Dr Julian Partridge.

So why does the outdated image of the explorer linger? It's a legacy from a time when whole swathes of territory were being revealed. The Victorian explorers were the heroes of their day.

continued ▶

continued

Exploration was something that happened not in a laboratory but in some godforsaken wilderness.

The most famous moment in the history of exploration is not the Russian Yuri Gagarin's launch into space – the first time man had escaped the bounds of our planet – but the finding of a 'lost' explorer by Stanley: "Dr Livingstone, I presume." The two men captured our imagination by greeting each other with a civilised handshake, symbolically uniting in the heart of the Dark Continent.

I asked a range of those whom we might think of as today's leading explorers how they define the word. According to Sir Ranulph Fiennes, who the *Guinness Book of Records* dubbed the "greatest living explorer", an explorer is "someone who has done something that no human has done before and also done something scientifically useful".

One of the leading mountaineers of the postwar generation, Sir Chris Bonington, feels exploration is to be found in the act of physically touching the unknown. "You have to have gone somewhere new," he says.

So, with the Victorian image of the heroic trailblazer reaching its use-by date, it would appear that it's time to widen the definition of an explorer. A worthy place to start is in the sciences, where the bounds of knowledge are being pushed back daily. Astronomers are using ever-larger and more sensitive telescopes to examine the farthest reaches of the cosmos, in effect looking billions of years back in time. Meanwhile, their colleagues are investigating the solar system, using remote-controlled probes to capture unprecedented images from the surface of Mars and beyond.

It seems that exploration is all about pushing back or examining a frontier of knowledge and then imparting the new information.

We are all explorers. Our desire to discover and to share our new-found knowledge are part of being human and have played a vital role in our success as a species.

By Benedict Allen from *Geographical*

What the writer thinks

1 Close read the first five paragraphs.

a What image of an explorer does the writer expect the reader to have?

b Why does the writer think this image of an explorer is out-of-date?

2 Close read the rest of the article.

a Write a definition of an explorer that you think the writer of this article would agree with.

b Discuss this definition with your partner and compare it with the 'Profile of an explorer' you prepared in the pre-reading activity. Are there any similarities between the two definitions?

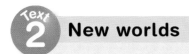

This text is from a novel about a fourteen-year-old boy, Alex, who has been taken by his grandmother, Kate, a writer, on an expedition up the Amazon River in search of a rare tribe of Indians and a mythical 'beast' (similar to the Loch Ness Monster). Here, Alex experiences for the first time what it is to be away from civilization as they travel up the Amazon.

Up the Amazon

The jungle loomed threateningly on both banks of the river. The captain's orders were clear: do not wander off for any reason; once among the trees, you lose your sense of direction. There were stories of foreigners who though only a few yards from the river had died without ever finding it. At dawn, they would see rosy dolphins leaping through the water and hundreds of birds flocking. They also saw the large aquatic mammals called manatees; the females of that species gave rise to the legend of the sirens. At night, they would see red dots in the dense growth along the banks, the eyes of caimans[1] peering through the dark.

Time went by slowly, hours dragging into eternity; even so, Alex was never bored. He would sit at the prow of the boat and observe nature, and read, and play his grandfather's flute. The jungle seemed to come alive and respond to the sound of the instrument; even the noisy crew and the passengers on the boat would fall silent and listen. Those were the only times that Kate paid any attention to Alex. The writer was a woman of few words; she spent her day reading or writing in her notebooks, and in general ignored Alex or treated him like any other member of the expedition. It was pointless to go to her and present a problem directly related to survival, such as food, health, or safety. She would look him up and down with obvious scorn, and answer that there are two kinds of problems: those that solve themselves and those that have no solution ... so please not to bother her with foolishness. It was good that his hand had healed rapidly, because otherwise she would be capable of solving the matter by suggesting he cut it off. (Kate was a woman of extreme measures.) She had loaned him maps and books about the Amazon so he could look things up for himself. If Alex commented on what he had read about the Indians, or outlined his theories about the Beast, she would reply, without taking her eyes from the page before her, 'Never lose an opportunity to keep your mouth shut, Alexander.'

[1]**caimans** – *animals found in South America related to crocodiles and alligators*

continued ▶

continued

Everything about this trip was so different from the world Alex had grown up in that he felt like a visitor from another galaxy. Now he had to do without comforts he had always taken for granted, like a bed, a bathroom, running water, and electricity. He used his grandmother's camera to take snapshots, in order to have proof to show back in California. His friends would never believe that he had held a three-foot-long alligator!

His most serious problem was food. He had always been a picky eater, and now they were serving him things he couldn't even name. All he could identify on the boat were canned beans, dried beef, and coffee, none of which he had a taste for. One day the crew shot a couple of monkeys, and that night when the boat was tied up along the riverbank they were roasted. They looked like a couple of burned infants, and Alex felt queasy just seeing them. The next morning they caught a *pirarucú*, an enormous fish that everyone but Alex, who didn't even taste it, thought was delicious. He had decided when he was three years old that he didn't like fish. His mother, weary of struggling to make him eat it, had given up, and from then on served him only food he liked. Which wasn't much. That short list kept him hungry the whole trip; all he had were bananas, a can of condensed milk, and several packages of crackers. It didn't seem to matter to his grandmother that he was hungry. Or to anyone else. No one paid any attention to him.

Several times a day a brief but torrential rain fell and the humidity was horrendous. Alex had to get used to the fact that his clothing never really got dry and that after the sun went down, they were attacked by clouds of mosquitoes. The foreigners' defense was to douse themselves in insect repellent – The *caboclos,* on the other hand, seemed immune to the bites.

On the third day, a radiant morning, they had to stop because there was a problem with the motor. While the captain tried to repair it, everyone else stretched out in the shade of the roof to rest. It was too hot to move, but Alex decided it was a perfect place to cool off. He jumped into the water, which looked as shallow as a bowl of soup, but he sank like a stone beneath the surface.

'Only an idiot tests the bottom with his feet,' Alex's grandmother commented when he came to the surface streaming water from his ears.

Alex swam away from the boat. He felt so comfortable that when something quickly brushed by his hand he took an instant to react. Not having any idea what kind of danger lay in store – maybe caimans didn't hug the riverbanks, after all – he began to swim as fast as he could back toward the boat, but he stopped short when he heard his grandmother yelling not to move. He obeyed out of habit, even though his instinct was advising the opposite. He floated as quietly as possible and then saw a huge fish at his side. He thought it was a shark, and his heart stopped, but the fish made a quick turn and came back, curious, coming so close that Alex could see its smile. This time his heart leaped, and he had to force himself not to shout with joy. He was swimming with a dolphin!

'Did you see, Kate? No one is going to believe this!' Alex yelled when he was back at the boat, so excited he could barely speak.

From *City of Beasts* by Isabel Allende

Looking at language

1 Skim read the first paragraph. How is the landscape depicted on their journey up the Amazon? Refer closely to the writer's use of language and choose three examples which help you to **see images**.

Interpreting the meanings

2 Skim read the text from the beginning of paragraph three *'Everything about this trip was so different ...'* to *'Did you see, Kate? No one is going to believe this!'*

   a What is Alex's reaction to his situation in this extract? What does Alex learn about himself on this journey? Try to **rationalise what is happening**.

   b What does Alex learn about the nature of exploration? Give evidence from the text to support your views.

Text 3 New worlds

This text is taken from an article which appeared in *The Guardian* newspaper in July, 2003. In this extract, the science editor, Tim Radford, discusses the discovery, by astronomers, of a planetary system very like our own.

Jim, our scans now show that life as we know it may exist in
100bn galaxies

Astronomers have pinpointed a planetary system which resembles our own solar system, raising hopes of the discovery of Earth-like planets capable of bearing life.

For the first time, they have identified a Jupiter-like planet, orbiting a star like the sun, at much the same distance from the parent star as Jupiter is from the sun.

The star, known only as HD70642, is 90 light years away in constellation Puppis. Scientists estimate this star is orbited, once every six years, by a planet about twice the mass of Jupiter. Jupiter – more massive than all its companion planets combined – takes 12 years to orbit the sun.

'This is the closest we have yet got to a real solar-system-like planet, and advances our search for systems that are even more like our own,' said Hugh Jones of Liverpool John Moores University, who announced the discovery yesterday at a conference on extrasolar planets in Paris.

Until 1995, there was no evidence at all of planets orbiting other stars. Since the first dramatic discovery eight years ago, researchers have identified more than 100 planetary systems within 150 light years of Earth.

No one has seen any of these planets: researchers infer the presence of an orbiting planet from a kind of wobble in the light from the parent star. The technique is reliable but has limitations. It can most easily detect star systems with an enormous planet, probably made of gas, in an elliptical orbit that moves very close to the parent star.

But this rules out the possibility of life as Captain James T Kirk and Mr Spock in the television series *Star Trek* might know it. No conceivable creature could survive on a giant planet, and the presence of such a monster so close to a star would rule out any chance of a small, rocky planet in the same orbit.

Earth is known to astronomers as a 'Goldilocks' planet, not so far away that water freezes, not so close that it boils: in fact, just right for life to evolve. The excitement over HD70642 is because its orbital system leaves room for a series of rocky planets much nearer the parent star. It is the first evidence so far that other stars could be encircled by planets like Earth.

Until yesterday's announcement, Earth, Mars and Venus seemed rare, or perhaps even unique. Now planets like them elsewhere in the galaxy are beginning to seem probable. But they still have to be identified. The chase is about to accelerate. The next step is a space-based telescope that can survey the sky for changes in the intensity of starlight as big planets transit across them. In 2008, a new generation of space telescopes will be powerful enough to detect the transit of Earth-sized planets.

And in 2015, Nasa and Europe could launch an entire flotilla of spacecraft, all capable of focusing with exquisite accuracy on stars most likely to have rocky planets in their inner zones, in the hope of seeing reflected planetary light directly – and of identifying the chemical signatures of water or oxygen or methane in their atmospheres. Evidence of all three, say the theoreticians, would be an indication of life.

'We are confident – but not overconfident – that we will find Earths,' said Dr Penny. 'Life is another thing: we don't know how life starts. We could be alone in the universe.'

From *The Guardian* July 4, 2003

Studying the structure

1 **a** Skim read the text and make a list of the key points from the article.

    b What view does the writer have of the subject? How is this view supported by the structure of the article?

What the writer thinks

2 Close read the text from *'Earth is known as a 'Goldilocks' planet …'* to the end.

    a How appropriate is 'Goldilocks' as a description of Earth in this context?

    b What questions does the article raise about the possibility of life on other planets?

    c What case does the writer make for space exploration of the future?

▶ Compare

You are now going to compare how the writers explore the theme of exploration in these three texts.

1 Skim read the three texts and then briefly describe the view of exploration shown in each text.

- Are there any similarities between the texts?
- What are the major differences?

Remember to give evidence from each text to support your comments.

2 Look again at Text 2: Up the Amazon, and compare this with the other two information texts. What features of language or style can you find which set this text apart from the other two texts? Discuss with a partner and find three examples from the text to support your ideas.

3 Under the title of each text, list the key points made for and against exploration. Collate all the information you have gathered from each extract and any other research on this subject and write a speech for a class debate on the motion:

'This house believes that exploration is a thing of the past.'

You may choose to propose or oppose the motion. Work in pairs and try out your speeches on one another as you go along.

Moving about

Introduction

It is hard to imagine a world without cars. Many people would consider owning a car to be a necessity. For some people cars are a status symbol and they dream of owning a Porsche or Lamborghini. For others, cars are an everyday reality helping to get them to work and back, taking the children to school and doing the supermarket run. The three texts that you will be reading in this unit present different perspectives on the role of the car in our society.

 Henry Ford   Driving Miss Phoebe   Transport 2000

Reading strategies

- make judgements
- infer
- establish a relationship with the writer
- empathise

Pre-reading: make judgements

1   In pairs, discuss the advantages and disadvantages of cars. Organise your ideas in a table like the one below:

Advantages of cars	Disadvantages of cars

2   Prepare a short speech where one of you presents the positive aspects and one of you presents the negative aspects. For the positive aspects you could consider issues of time and convenience, for example. For the negative aspects you could consider environmental issues and road safety. You should support your points with clear examples.

Text 1 Moving about

Henry Ford can be credited with starting the mass production of the motor car in America with his car called the Model T. Almost a hundred years later the Ford brand is still going strong with the Ford Focus being a popular family car that you may have seen advertised or on the roads today. This information text recounts Henry Ford's achievements.

Henry Ford

Henry Ford changed the face of the modern world. The founder of the Ford Motor Company, Henry Ford revolutionized the auto industry with his proclamation 'I will build a car for the great multitude.' From this simple desire to create a car that the ordinary man or woman could afford came great changes in industry, society and even in the lifestyles we all live today.

In 1908 the Ford Motor Company began production of their Everyman car – the Model T. This automobile initiated a new era in personal transportation. It was easy to operate, maintain, and could handle the rough roads and rutted tracks that horse-drawn vehicles used.

Initially, the Model T's price of $850 was too high for many customers; so in order to increase profitability and lower the price Henry Ford created a moving assembly line method of construction for his new car. This system helped to reduce the assembly time of the Model T from about $12\frac{1}{2}$ hours to $1\frac{1}{2}$ hours. As the time it took to build the car fell so did the price.

Henry Ford's innovations didn't stop there. He doubled his factory workers' wages and cut their working hours from nine to eight hours in order to create a three-shift workday. These mass-production techniques would eventually allow for the manufacture of a Model T every 24 seconds. To further encourage productivity, Henry Ford introduced a profit-sharing plan, which set aside part of the company's profits for its employees. He argued that good pay made for good workers, and his well paid workers could afford to buy more cars – Ford cars. Demand for the affordable car soared even as production went up and millions of men poured into Detroit to try to gain employment at the enormous Ford manufacturing plant. The Model T was hailed by the American public as a dream machine and Henry Ford was the creator of that dream.

But Henry Ford wasn't just content with building the perfect car for the American man and woman; he dreamed of transforming the landscape in which they drove it. His vision showed Ford dealerships across the country selling and repairing his cars, petrol stations in every town fuelling them and a network of safer, faster roads on which they could drive. With his usual single-minded determination and crusading zeal, Henry Ford worked to turn his dreams into reality.

The advent of the Model T seemed to renew a sense of independence among Americans. With more people out on the roads, many roads were now being paved and highways and bridges were being built for cars. Access to places was easier now, which led to the building of more shops, restaurants and businesses. Henry Ford had transformed the nation's way of life and created a population entranced with the possibility of going anywhere at anytime.

By making cheap cars for the ordinary people, Henry Ford had helped to make great changes to society. This new society was an urban one, where people had higher wages and more free time in which to spend them.

Interpreting the meanings and what the writer thinks

1 a Close read the article. **Establish a relationship with the writer.** What clues are there in the text about the writer's attitude towards Henry Ford? You should consider:

- the language the writer uses to describe Henry Ford
- the reasons he suggests for Ford's success.

b What impression do you get of Henry Ford from this article? Give reasons for your answer. **Make judgements**. In your opinion, do you think Henry Ford 'changed the face of the modern world'?

Moving about

Do your parents drive you to school, or do you use public transport or walk? In this article, which appeared in the Automobile Association (AA) magazine, the comedienne Jenny Eclair reflects in a light hearted way on the pros and cons of doing the school run as a parent.

Driving Miss Phoebe

12 years of stale crisps, dog poo and war on the back seat ... but Jenny Eclair still loves driving her daughter

Twelve years, two Golfs, a Daimler and a Polo, three wing mirrors, a million quaint Anglo Saxon swear words, thousands of mouldy apple cores and a billion dropped crisps ... You can always tell which is the school-run car by its smell. At times, my various cars have smelt very bad indeed – so much so that my daughter regularly used to faint on her way to nursery school.

That's when it started, when she was two and her kindergarten was at the top of a very steep hill. I could have wheeled her up in her buggy, but, let's face it, I'd have had to keep sitting down for a rest and she wouldn't have got there till lunchtime. So, I drove her, and I'm still driving her.

I must be mad. She's 14, she has two working legs (albeit skinny ones), surely she could walk? Walk! She's a teenager; teenage girls can't walk. They haven't got any muscle tone – all they do is watch television. They're like jellyfish with blackheads. Mine is so lazy she recently turned round and said, "Mum. I'm tired. Will you watch *ER* for me?"

Who'd choose to walk?

To be honest, I don't blame her for not wanting to walk. I hate walking, all that putting one leg in front of another, over and over again. So tedious. Anyway, it's not as if her secondary school is a nice walk away, over babbling brooks and meadows. It's an urban trek, not only up a very steep hill, but down the hill and round the corner. She'd never make it. I'd put more money on a salmon.

When I was her age, I rode a bike to school. Every limb would have to have fallen off – and believe me, I tried – before my mother would have dreamt of backing her orange Mini out of the garage. Come hailstorms or blizzards, in a flapping gabardine mac, my fat little knees would pump furiously a mile there and a mile back, a pocketful of sherbet lemons keeping me going.

How about a donkey?

Phoebe doesn't ride a bike; she'd have to wear a helmet, because we live in London, and that would ruin her hair! She could get a bus, if they went in vaguely the right direction – but they don't. In fact, considering the amount of clobber she has to carry the only solution (apart from me giving her a lift, of course) would be a donkey.

OK, I'm making excuses; we live in a rough area, she can't run very fast ...

The fact is, I like taking her. The school run delivers 15 precious minutes of 'us' time, to gossip, bitch and natter. No-one else can make me laugh as much as she can before nine o'clock in the morning. And the fact that I've got a coat on over my pyjamas is irrelevant.

Actually, this current school run is a breeze – now that she is no longer three, I don't have to carry her screaming into the car (unless she's got double Physics, of course). Neither do I have to drive very far: Camberwell to Dulwich – barely gets me out of second gear (yes, I'm one of 'those' drivers).

Armageddon on the back seat

The worse school run was the primary school leg where, every term day for seven years, we made the seven-mile round trip from the bowels of South London over the river to Chelsea! Why? Because the local schools were full of people biting each other and screaming (and that was the teachers).

It wasn't just us, either, the Chelsea run involved three other local kids, so at least the burden was shared among the parents. Ha! My partner was the only dad who ever braved it. And that's not surprising, really; we did have some nutters on board.

Most days, Armageddon would break out on the back seat: "He pinched me!" "She kicked me!" In the end I discovered that I could drown them out with old punk tapes. Seven-year-olds really like John Cooper Clarke and The Clash. I'd regularly deposit them outside school chanting *London's Burning* – and it wasn't the nursery rhyme version.

No school run is drama-free. There's always one child who climbs into the car with a heavily dog-poo-encrusted shoe; there's never anywhere to park; other mothers are bitches from hell; and I once

drove over a lollipop man's foot. But at least it's all accomplished before the sun's over the yardarm.

The dreaded disco run

Much more inconvenient is when the school run morphs into the disco run. Last month, my daughter and her cronies went to a massive teenage thrash in Hammersmith: pick-up time 1.30am! Sober and exhausted, her father and I waited outside on the pavement with all the other wheyfaced parents (Sir Bob Geldof included). And all of a sudden, I regressed. I felt exactly like I had on that first day I'd picked her up from nursery: "Has she had a good time? What if she comes out crying? What if a nasty boy's been mean to her?" Oh God, when does it end? I suppose when they're old enough to drive themselves.

The other day I remarked that, by the time she's 17, my Golf will be very clapped-out indeed and, depending on GCSE results and as long as she hasn't made me a grandmother, she just might inherit it. You should have seen her face: "Actually, Mum. I was thinking more along the lines of one of those new Minis!" "Get out," I said.

Yes, the school run can indeed be a nightmare, but I will miss it.

From AA magazine

137

How the reader feels

1 In your opinion, what are the advantages and disadvantages of:

- being driven to school
- taking public transport
- walking to school?

Looking at language

2 Close read the text. The narrative voice is a humorous one; the writer is trying to make a serious point in an amusing way.

   a How does the writer use humour to convey her point of view? Scan the text, picking out examples of the following types of humour:

- irony (eg *'teenage girls can't walk'*)
- self deprecation (eg *'yes, I'm one of 'those' drivers'*)
- exaggeration
- rhetorical devices.

   b How does the writer achieve an informal tone? Consider the use of:

- colloquialisms (eg *'natter'*)
- asides (eg *'To be honest …'*)
- use of parenthesis
- punctuation.

Scan the text, finding examples of where these techniques have been used.

Moving about

The following text is posted on Transport 2000's website. Transport 2000 is an independent national organisation that aims to encourage less use of cars and more use of public transport, walking and cycling. It states on its website that its vision 'is of a country where traffic no longer dominates our lives'.

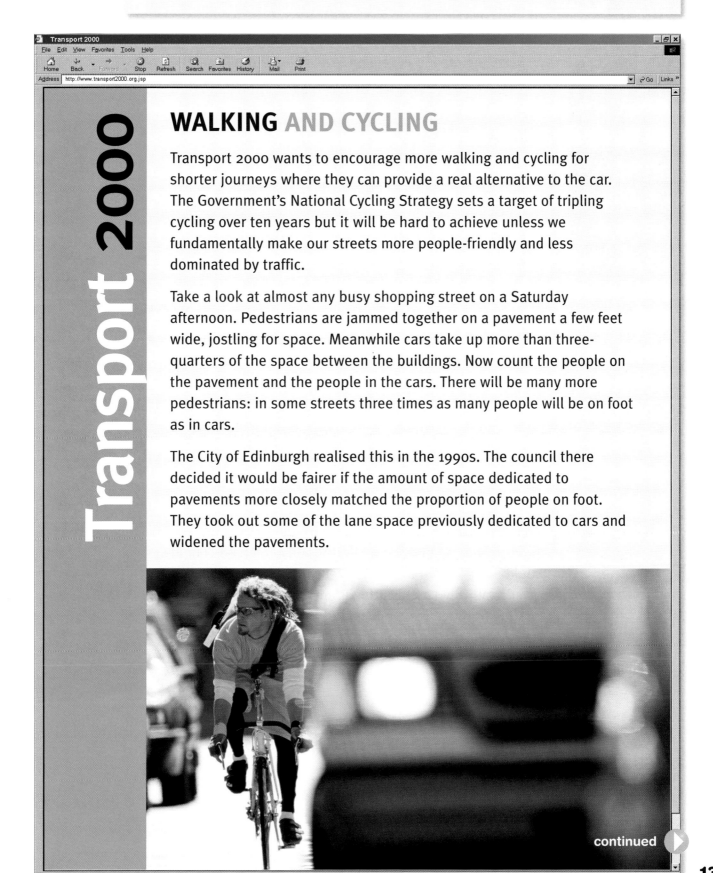

WALKING AND CYCLING

Transport 2000 wants to encourage more walking and cycling for shorter journeys where they can provide a real alternative to the car. The Government's National Cycling Strategy sets a target of tripling cycling over ten years but it will be hard to achieve unless we fundamentally make our streets more people-friendly and less dominated by traffic.

Take a look at almost any busy shopping street on a Saturday afternoon. Pedestrians are jammed together on a pavement a few feet wide, jostling for space. Meanwhile cars take up more than three-quarters of the space between the buildings. Now count the people on the pavement and the people in the cars. There will be many more pedestrians: in some streets three times as many people will be on foot as in cars.

The City of Edinburgh realised this in the 1990s. The council there decided it would be fairer if the amount of space dedicated to pavements more closely matched the proportion of people on foot. They took out some of the lane space previously dedicated to cars and widened the pavements.

continued ▶

continued

Transport 2000

File Edit View Favorites Tools Help

Home   Back   Forward   Stop   Refresh   Search   Favorites   History   Mail   Print

Address http://www.transport2000.org.jsp   Go   Links

This is just one practical step to make walking safer and more pleasant. Transport 2000's checklist for foot-friendly streets offers some more:

- Provide good crossings where people actually want to cross.
- Raise the road to pavement level at junctions.
- Remove guard rails, which encourage motorists to drive faster.
- Civilise residential streets by creating 20mph zones and Home Zones.
- Cut speeds on busy main roads where there are also shops, homes, parks and other places people may wish to visit on foot.
- Crack down on illegal pavement parking, with tough enforcement.
- Create an attractive environment, with greenery, art and good design.
- Provide benches for people to take a break and watch the world go by.
- Keep streets clean and well maintained.
- Get rid of pedestrian subways and bridges and replace them with surface level crossings.

We also need to make our streets bike-friendly. For short journeys of a few miles, cycling is often quicker than driving. It also keeps you healthy, lets you breathe the fresh air (or at least, fresher air than motorists: surveys show drivers in busy traffic are exposed to high pollution levels because they are sitting in a tunnel of fumes), and keeps you in touch with your local neighbourhood.

Many people are reluctant to cycle because of the danger from high traffic speeds. In built-up areas, properly enforced 20mph speed limits would make it safer and more pleasant to get to places by bike. The lower limit would make little difference to drivers' journey times. Tackling traffic congestion and keeping heavy lorries off unsuitable roads would also improve the street environment for cycling. Continuous, high quality cycle lanes and a properly signed backstreet cycle network would also make cycling more attractive. Employers can help encourage cycling by providing lockers, changing facilities, and covered cycle parking. Schools have a vital role to play: by working with local councils to make it safe and easy for pupils to cycle to school, they can help nurture a culture of cycling and give children a good start in life as healthy, active citizens.

From Transport 2000

Done   Internet

Interpreting the meanings

1 Close read the second paragraph.

    a What argument is put across here?

    b How does the second paragraph try to appeal directly to the reader?

Explaining the ideas

2 Close read the rest of the article.

    a What transport issues are Transport 2000 trying to address? Scan the article, making a list of the key points.

    b Read closely from *'We also need to make...'* to the end of the text. Produce a bullet point checklist for making cycling *'safer and more pleasant'*.

 Compare

You are now going to compare the presentation of views on the motor car in the Text 1: Henry Ford and Text 3: Transport 2000.

Working in groups, prepare an improvisation and role play. Imagine that you are presenting a current affairs programme on the theme of transport. The focus of your programme is the question: 'Is the car an essential part of twenty-first century life?' Two of your guests on the programme will be the Managing Director of a car company and a representative from Transport 2000.

Prepare an improvisation where each of these two guests is interviewed to give their views on the question: 'Is the car an essential part of twenty-first century life?' Your improvisation could also include your own views on what you consider to be the future of transport for the twenty-first century.

You should refer closely to the information in Texts 1 and 3 to help you devise a convincing interview. You should consider:

The view of the motor car presented in each text
- Is the view positive or negative?

The attitude of the writer of each text
- What is the writer's attitude towards the motor car in the Henry Ford text?
- What is Transport 2000's attitude towards the effect of the motor car?

The tone of each text and how this is matched to its purpose
- Think about the tone of Text 1.

Why do you think the writer has adopted this tone?
- What is the tone of Text 3? What are the reasons for this tone?

Their different visions of the future of transport
- What was Henry Ford's vision for the motor car?
- What is Transport 2000 campaigning for?

Introduction

Heroes have always been important: as historical characters, fictional 'larger-than-life' figures and role models. Although there is a vast difference between Superman and Mother Theresa, there are 'heroic' qualities shared by both individuals, such as a driving force to 'do good', a dedication to duty, compassion for others and strength of character. These three texts deal with three very different heroic figures, yet also show how they share some common characteristics.

 Text 1 The coming of King Arthur

 Text 2 Sir Thomas More

 Text 3 Ellen MacArthur

Reading strategies

- ask questions
- make judgements
- deduce
- interpret patterns
- see images
- infer
- relate to previous reading experience

Pre-reading: relate to previous reading experience

1 Think about three characters you admire and would call 'heroes'. Try to make them as different as possible – eg one from the present day, one from the past and one from fiction (book, TV programme or film). For each of them, note the qualities which make them heroic.

2 Compare your responses with others in your group. What similarities or differences are there? Are the choices of the boys different from those of the girls?

3 Discuss why heroes are so popular in books, films and TV programmes. Which fictional character chosen do you think is the most heroic figure?

KINGFISHER
challenge 2000

Heroes

King Arthur and his knights of the round table are one of the most important British legends. The story of King Arthur has come to represent the pinnacle of heroic and honourable behaviour. This text is an extract from a much longer poem by Alfred Lord Tennyson. Here, Tennyson writes about the coronation of King Arthur.

THE COMING OF ARTHUR

'O King,' she cried, 'and I will tell thee: few,
Few, but all brave, all of one mind with him;
For I was near him when the savage yells
Of Uther's peerage died, and Arthur sat
Crown'd on the daïs, and his warriors cried,
"Be thou the king, and we will work thy will
Who love thee." Then the King in low deep tones
And simple words of great authority,
Bound them by so strait vows to his own self,
That when they rose, knighted from kneeling, some
Were pale as at the passing of a ghost,
Some flush'd, and others dazed, as one who wakes
Half-blinded at the coming of a light.

'But when he spake and cheer'd his Table Round
With large, divine, and comfortable words,
Beyond my tongue to tell thee – I beheld
From eye to eye thro' all their Order flash
A momentary likeness of the King:
And ere it left their faces, thro' the cross
And those around it and the Crucified,
Down from the casement over Arthur, smote
Flame-colour, vert and azure, in three rays,
One falling upon each of three fair queens,
Who stood in silence near his throne, the friends
Of Arthur, gazing on him, tall, with bright
Sweet faces, who will help him at his need.

'And there I saw mage Merlin, whose vast wit
And hundred winters are but as the hands
Of loyal vassals[1] toiling for their liege[2].
'And near him stood the Lady of the Lake,
Who knows a subtler magic than his own –

[1]**vassals** – *subjects*   [2]**liege** – *Lord*

continued

continued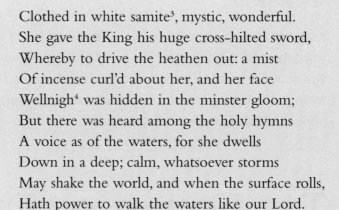

Clothed in white samite[3], mystic, wonderful.
She gave the King his huge cross-hilted sword,
Whereby to drive the heathen out: a mist
Of incense curl'd about her, and her face
Wellnigh[4] was hidden in the minster gloom;
But there was heard among the holy hymns
A voice as of the waters, for she dwells
Down in a deep; calm, whatsoever storms
May shake the world, and when the surface rolls,
Hath power to walk the waters like our Lord.

'There likewise I beheld Excalibur
Before him at his crowning borne, the sword
That rose from out the bosom of the lake,
And Arthur row'd across and took it – rich
With jewels, elfin Urim, on the hilt,
Bewildering heart and eye – the blade so bright
That men are blinded by it – on one side,
Graven in the oldest tongue of all this world,
"Take me," but turn the blade and ye shall see,
And written in the speech ye speak yourself,
"Cast me away!" And sad was Arthur's face
Taking it, but old Merlin counsell'd him,
"Take thou and strike! the time to cast away
Is yet far-off." So this great brand the king
Took, and by this will beat his foemen down.'

From *Idylls of the King* by Alfred Lord Tennyson

[3]**samite** – *silk*
[4]**Wellnigh** – *soon*

Looking at language

1   Scan the text for the language that describes King Arthur.

   a   What qualities are attributed to King Arthur? You might look at:

   - his behaviour
   - his effect on others
   - the narrative voice
   - the way King Arthur is explicitly described.

   b   **Deduce** what this text tells us about King Arthur as a person.

Interpreting the meanings

2   Close read the section about the Lady of the Lake from *'And near him stood the Lady of the Lake'* to *'Hath power to walk the waters like our Lord.'* How are her mystical qualities developed? You might consider:

   - the images used
   - the use of punctuation
   - the line structure
   - any patterns of language.

Heroes

Text 2

Sir Thomas More was a devout sixteenth-century Catholic statesman who became a martyr to his religious faith. When Henry VIII wanted to marry Anne Boleyn, Sir Thomas More was against it. Henry was already married and divorce was strictly forbidden by the Catholic church. As a result of his continued opposition, Sir Thomas More was beheaded for treason. The following text consists of a history website giving information about Sir Thomas More and the letter written by him before his execution.

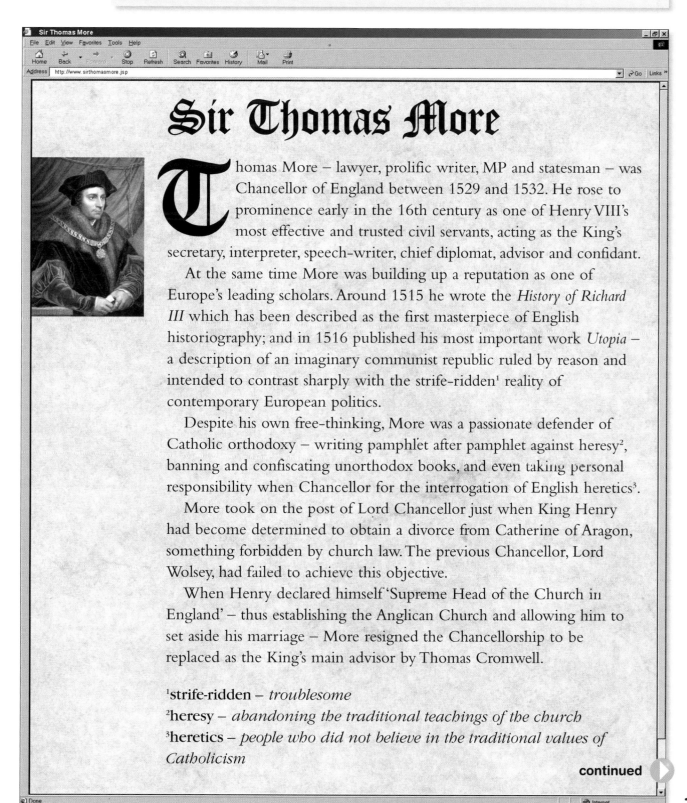

Sir Thomas More

Thomas More – lawyer, prolific writer, MP and statesman – was Chancellor of England between 1529 and 1532. He rose to prominence early in the 16th century as one of Henry VIII's most effective and trusted civil servants, acting as the King's secretary, interpreter, speech-writer, chief diplomat, advisor and confidant.

At the same time More was building up a reputation as one of Europe's leading scholars. Around 1515 he wrote the *History of Richard III* which has been described as the first masterpiece of English historiography; and in 1516 published his most important work *Utopia* – a description of an imaginary communist republic ruled by reason and intended to contrast sharply with the strife-ridden[1] reality of contemporary European politics.

Despite his own free-thinking, More was a passionate defender of Catholic orthodoxy – writing pamphlet after pamphlet against heresy[2], banning and confiscating unorthodox books, and even taking personal responsibility when Chancellor for the interrogation of English heretics[3].

More took on the post of Lord Chancellor just when King Henry had become determined to obtain a divorce from Catherine of Aragon, something forbidden by church law. The previous Chancellor, Lord Wolsey, had failed to achieve this objective.

When Henry declared himself 'Supreme Head of the Church in England' – thus establishing the Anglican Church and allowing him to set aside his marriage – More resigned the Chancellorship to be replaced as the King's main advisor by Thomas Cromwell.

[1]**strife-ridden** – *troublesome*
[2]**heresy** – *abandoning the traditional teachings of the church*
[3]**heretics** – *people who did not believe in the traditional values of Catholicism*

continued

continued

He continued to argue against the King's divorce and the split with Rome[4], and in 1534 was arrested after refusing to swear an Oath of Succession repudiating[5] the Pope and accepting the annulment of the marriage to Catherine. Fifteen months later More was tried for treason at Westminster, and on July 6th 1535 he was executed by beheading on Tower Hill.

The following letter was written by Thomas More to his daughter Margaret from the Tower of London; it was written with a stick of charcoal on 5 July 1535, the day before his execution.

Our Lord bless you, good daughter, and your good husband, and your little boy, and all yours, and all my children, and all my god-children and all our friends. Recommend me when ye may to my good daughter Cecily, whom I beseech[6] Our Lord to comfort; and I send her my blessing and to all her children, and pray her to pray for me. I send her a handkercher[7], and God comfort my good son, her husband. My good daughter Daunce hath the picture in parchment that you delivered me from my Lady Coniers, her name on the back. Show her that I heartily pray her that you may send it in my name to her again, for a token from me to pray for me.

I cumber[8] you, good Margaret much, but I would be sorry if it should be any longer than to-morrow, for it is St Thomas's even[9], and the utas[10] of St Peter; and therefore, to-morrow long I to go to God. It were a day very meet and convenient for me.

I never liked your manner towards me better than when you kissed me last; for I love when daughterly love and dear charity hath no leisure to look to worldly courtesy. Farewell, my dear child, and pray for me, and I shall for you and all your friends, that we may merrily meet in heaven. I thank you for your great cost. I pray you at time convenient recommend me to my good son John More. Our Lord bless him and his good wife, my loving daughter, to whom I pray him to be good, as he hath great cause; and that, if the land of mine come to his hands, he break not my will concerning his sister Daunce. And the Lord bless Thomas and Austin, and all that they shall have.

From BBC history website

[4]**Rome** – *the Catholic Church* [5]**repudiating** – *disowning*
[6]**beseech** – *beg* [7]**handkercher** – *hankerchief* [8]**cumber** – *burden*
[9]**even** – *evening* [10]**utas** – *eight days after the feast of St Peter*

Interpreting the meanings

1 This text is made up of two different sources. The first part of the text is a secondary historical source, providing background information, whereas the letter is a primary historical source.

    a Close read both sources and **ask questions** of the text. Working in pairs, discuss what we gain as readers from the two different sources. You might consider:

- the writer's viewpoint
- the writer's purpose
- the tone of the writing
- specific language features and their effect
- the audience of each source
- the effect on the reader.

    b Prepare notes under these headings and present your notes as a table on a blank OHT for the rest of the class to read and discuss.

Looking at language

2 Close read Thomas More's letter. What impression do you get of him and what can you **infer** about his relationship with his daughter? You might consider:

- the context in which the letter is written
- the way in which he addresses his daughter
- the advice and messages he sends
- his attitude towards his family
- the way his belief in God is shown.

3 Heroes

Have you ever taken on a challenge that depended on nothing but your own individual talents and resources? Ellen MacArthur proved that she was a true hero by sailing single-handedly around the world. This text is taken from Ellen MacArthur's personal website.

Ellen MacArthur

File Edit View Favorites Tools Help

Home　Back　Forward　Stop　Refresh　Search　Favorites　History　Mail　Print

Address http://www.ellenmacarthur.com/jsp

You can make it happen

There would be nothing remarkable in Derbyshire producing a Hill Walker of the Year or even a Potholer of the Year. But for this landlocked county to produce Yachtsman of the Year, and for that award to go to a 22-year-old slip of a girl from Whatstandwell, is nothing short of miraculous.

Ellen MacArthur does not come from any yachting club, 'Howard's Way' culture and has not risen through the ranks of the sailing elite. As she cheerfully puts it: "I'm not a cool racing person with the right designer gear." For Cowes and Hamble, substitute Flash Dam and Ogston Reservoir. Her great-grandparents came from Skye and were boating people and a great-uncle ran away to sea when young, but any real connection with the sea is tenuous. When Ellen was eight, an aunt took her sailing on the east coast, after which she was hooked.

At school, she saved up all her dinner money for three years to buy her first boat, an eight-foot dinghy. She was a "geek", she says candidly, spending all her spare time reading sailing books in the library and soaking up information like a sponge. She was going to be a vet but a bout of glandular fever while she was in the Sixth Form set her back. Instead, she resolved to become a professional sailor.

So at 18, she sailed single-handed round Britain and won the Young Sailor of the Year award for being the youngest person to pass the Yachtmaster Offshore Qualification, with the highest possible marks. The nautical establishment looked on benignly[1] at 'Little Ellen' from Derbyshire, just 5' 2" tall, and metaphorically patted her on the head. She wrote 2,500 letters to potential sponsors – and received just two replies.

They stopped patting her on the head and looked at her in a new light when she undertook the Mini-Transat solo race from Brest in France to Martinique in the French Caribbean in 1997. With little money, no major sponsorship and not even a return ticket, she took the ferry to France, bought Le Poisson, a 21ft yacht, and refitted it on site. She learned French in order to deal with French shipwrights and camped next to Le Poisson while she worked on the mast and hull.

Then she sailed 2,700 miles across the Atlantic, a race which she completed in 33 days. This achievement brought her first major

[1]benignly – *mildly*

sponsorship from Kingfisher, who believe in backing young people with an ambition to succeed. In a new boat, the 50ft Kingfisher, she undertook the Route du Rhum transatlantic race in November of last year, winning her class and finishing fifth overall.

She is a heroine in France, where she has been named 'La Jeune Espoire de la Voile' (Sailing's Young Hope). More people flock down to the quayside to see her off on a race than fill Wembley Stadium for a Cup Final. They shout her favourite phrase, "Ellen à donf' which means "Full on! Go for it". Sailing in France is what the marine industry hopes will arrive in Britain, where water sports appeal to a wider audience, especially young people.

Thousands follow Ellen's race progress on the Internet. Messages and digital pictures from a boat in the middle of the Atlantic can be instantly relayed around the world from the onboard computer and updated every hour. Satellite phones mean contact on shore for weather routing and emergencies. Ellen's uncle, Dr Glyn MacArthur, a GP in Crich, was woken during one night to hear Ellen's voice asking his advice on a head injury she'd sustained during a severe gale on the Route du Rhum.

Exhausting racing conditions mean sleeping in ten-minute snatches, a survival suit that doesn't come off for a week at a time and hands and wrists covered in salt sores and cuts. Dehydrated food comes in packets: if they get wet, the labels peel off and she doesn't know if she'll be eating curry or pudding until she opens one. Sails, weighing twice as much as she does, may need changing a dozen times a day.

There are moments of pure elation – sunrises and seascapes that take the breath away. But there are nightmare times when lone sailors must become engineers.

She describes a night and day that ran together, when 15 litres of fluid (resembling cooking oil) burst from the rams controlling the keel, the big steel fin that goes down through the boat. In heavy seas, slipping and sliding round the deck and with the keel unstabilised, she had to drip feed oil back in to the reservoir through a tiny funnel. Before she'd fixed the keel, a piece on one of the sails ripped, which meant taking down the sail and sewing for five hours through the night. Water came through the hatch and was swilling round the boat. And then later, when she'd dried all the compartments, a mighty bang threw the boat on to its side and all the electricity that powered the satcom communication system went off.

What keeps her going is sheer determination not to be beaten: "When it's a race, you just can't stop. Five times a day, you get the position of all the other boats in the race and work out whether you've gained or lost time," she says. "It would be easy to say, 'chill out', when you're tired but you never have to lose the goal of the finish line. That's what you set out to do and that's what you stick to."

From www.ellenmacarthur.com

Studying the structure

1 How is the information in this text organised and presented? You should comment on:

- the headline
- the layout
- the use of images
- Ellen MacArthur's own testimony (evidence)
- the links made between paragraphs.

Interpreting the meanings

2 What impression do you get of Ellen MacArthur from this text? Is she a typical hero? Support your answers with close reference to the text.

▶ Compare

You are now going to compare the nature of heroism as shown in these three texts. Make notes on the different heroic qualities shown by the three protagonists (King Arthur, Sir Thomas More and Ellen MacArthur) by considering the following questions.

1 Consider the ways in which the stories are narrated. Think about:

- the purpose of the text
- the audience
- the writer's viewpoint
- the language used to describe the heroic figures.

2 Think about the use of testimony in each of the texts. How does it help to create an image of heroism?

3 How typical are each of these protagonists as heroes? Consider the following heroic qualities and explain how the protagonists show these:

- doing good deeds
- bravery
- dedication
- personal sacrifice and hardship
- honour
- other personal attributes.

Remember to support your points with evidence from the texts.

4 Finally, explain which hero you admire the most and why.

16 Places worth saving

Introduction

You live in a fast moving world. Each day your local area is changing – new shops, new roads, new buildings. It happens so fast it's easy to forget what was there before – and harder still to remember if it was worth saving. The writers of the texts you are going to read are writing about places they believe are worth protecting for the future.

 Text 1 Ancient coral reefs under attack

 Text 2 The Galapagos

 Text 3 Going, Going

Reading strategies

- predict what will happen
- see images
- empathise
- make judgements

- relate to previous reading experience
- establish a relationship with the writer
- deduce
- reinterpret

Pre-reading: prediction

1 Before you read the first text, you are going to **make some predictions** about it. Predicting means:

- using what you already know about the subject to work out what the writing might be about

- **using your past reading experience** to work out how this kind of writing is usually structured

- looking for clues which suggest how the writing is going to develop.

Read the heading and the first two paragraphs of Text 1 about coral reefs and predict:

a What is the writer's attitude to the subject of coral reefs going to be?

b Where might this piece of writing appear?

c What information do you think the text will include?

You are going to read an article from an internet newsroom set up by the WWF. It combines information about coral reefs with explanations about how they are being damaged and descriptions of the impact of that damage.

Coral reefs

File Edit View Favorites Tools Help

Home   Back   Forward   Stop   Refresh   Search   Favorites   History   Mail   Print

Address   www.wwf.coralreefs.jsp

Ancient coral reefs under attack By Joanna Benn

Imagine a giant bulldozer crashing through the Amazon rainforest, demolishing trees, crushing animals, destroying living systems that are thousands of years old, all in a matter of hours.

The equivalent of this is happening on the deep ocean floor, to ancient coral reefs whose mysteries are only just beginning to be revealed.

These are not the tropical reefs that we are all familiar with, but cold-water coral – living as deep as 2000m below the ocean surface, well beyond the reach of sunlight and where the temperature can be as low as 4°C.

Despite their dark, chilly location, these reefs are every bit as beautiful as their tropical counterparts. The *Lophelia pertusa* reefs off the coasts of Scotland, Ireland, and Norway, for example, grow as delicate branches ranging in colour from orange to pink to white. Like tropical reefs, they are home to a multitude of other animals, including starfish, sea urchins, anemones, sponges, worms, and crabs. They are also likely to be important spawning and nursery grounds for several fish species, including commercially valuable ones.

Cold-water corals are also incredibly slow growing: it can take 40 years for a coral tree to become just 2cm thick. The largest reefs discovered so far are up to 3km wide and 45km long and are at least 4,500 years old – amongst the oldest living systems on the planet.

Although fishermen have known of their existence for a long time, it's only in the last decade or so that scientists have really started to study cold-water coral. They have been found around the world, from the Bering Sea and northern Europe to Florida, the Galapagos Islands, the southern Pacific, and even Antarctica.

Done

Internet

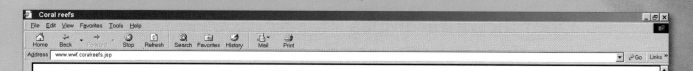

Coral reefs
File Edit View Favorites Tools Help
Home Back Forward Stop Refresh Search Favorites History Mail Print
Address www.wwf.coralreefs.jsp

Most deep-water reefs are poorly mapped, and it's likely that many more remain to be discovered. Many mysteries remain even for the best-studied reefs, including the details of how the corals feed and reproduce.

Alarmingly, the chance to investigate these unique ecosystems further is disappearing.

Industrial trawlers, whose huge nets capture nearly everything in their path, once avoided coral reefs and other rocky regions of the ocean floor because their nets would snag and tear. But the introduction of rockhopper trawls in the 1980s changed this. These trawls are fitted with large rubber tires or rollers that allow the net to pass easily over any rough surface. The largest, with heavy rollers over 75cm (30 inches) in diameter, are very powerful, capable of moving boulders weighing 25 tons. Now, there is virtually no part of the ocean floor that can't be trawled.

Not surprisingly, these trawls – whose use is now widespread – are extremely damaging to fragile and slow-growing structures like coral reefs.

"Rockhopper gear smashes reefs and other vulnerable habitats and species," says Dr Jan Helge Fosså from Norway's Institute of Marine Research. "Bottom trawling is the worst threat against biodiversity in the deep sea."

In an experiment off Alaska, 55 per cent of cold-water coral damaged by one pass of a trawl had not recovered a year later. Scars up to four kilometres long have been found in the reefs of the north-east Atlantic Ocean. And in heavily fished areas around coral seamounts off southern Australia, 90 per cent of the surfaces where coral used to grow are now bare rock.

The loss is not only a biological one. Cold-water corals are important habitats for already overexploited fish populations. Loss of fish nurseries through reef destruction translates into economic loss for the fishing industry. This loss could also affect food security.

"Much attention has been focused on the protection of tropical corals for their importance to fisheries, biodiversity, and for the economic benefits they bring to people, but cold-water corals are by no means less important," says Dr Simon Cripps, Director of WWF's Endangered Seas Programme. "Increased research and better protection are urgently needed to prevent these fragile and slow-growing habitats from being irreparably damaged."

"Cold-water corals are not only extraordinarily beautiful, but also important for the biodiversity of the deep sea," says Jan Helge Fosså. "And there's still so much to discover about them. Damaging bottom trawling must be stopped in areas where these corals live – if we destroy the reefs. then they're gone forever ..."

From the WWF Newsroom

Done   Internet

What the writer thinks

1 **a** What **images do you see** in your mind when you read the line *'Imagine a giant bulldozer crashing through the Amazonian rainforest...'*? Why does the writer begin the passage by asking the reader to do this?

   b Read the text closely and try to **establish a relationship with the writer**. Summarise:
   - the reasons the writer believes the coral reefs are worth saving
   - the threats the writer believes that they face.

2 The writer is presenting a particular viewpoint about the destruction of cold-water coral reefs. Close read the text to find evidence of the following strategies used by the writer to establish her point of view and influence her readers.

   - the use of emotive language to influence the reader
   - the use of complex sentences to provide a very detailed picture of the underwater landscape
   - the use of informal language to appeal more directly to the reader
   - the use of poetic language to persuade the reader of the value of the reefs.

   Use quotations and give evidence from the whole text to back up your answers.

Text 2

Places worth saving

Long before any writer imagined a Jurassic Park, in which dinosaurs were reincarnated, the Galapagos Islands were in existence – for real. Remote, volcanic, and uninhabited by people, the islands are even now caught in a time warp. Giant tortoises patrol fields of lava and dine on huge and ancient cactus plants. Charles Darwin found the Galapagos as fascinating as many tourists do today and recorded his thoughts in a detailed diary, an extract from which you are about to read.

The Galapagos

In the morning we landed on Chatham Island, which, like the others, rises with a tame and rounded outline, broken here and there by scattered hillocks, the remains of former craters. Nothing could be less inviting than the first appearance. A broken field of black basaltic lava, thrown into the most rugged waves, and crossed by great fissures[1], is everywhere covered by stunted, sun-burnt brushwood, which shows little signs of life. The dry and parched surface, being heated by the noon-day sun, gave to the air a close and sultry feeling, like that from a stove: we fancied even that the bushes smelt unpleasantly. Although I diligently tried to collect as many plants as possible, I succeeded in getting very few; and such wretched-looking little weeds would have better become an arctic than an equatorial Flora. The brushwood appears, from a short distance, as leafless as our trees during winter, and it was some time before I discovered that not only almost every plant was now in full leaf, but that the greater number were in flower. The commonest bush is one of the Euphorbiaceae: an acacia and a great odd-looking cactus are the only trees which afford any shade. After the season of heavy rains, the islands are said to appear for a short time partially green. The volcanic island of Fernando Noronha, placed in many respects under nearly similar conditions, is the only other country where I have seen a vegetation at all like this of the Galapagos Islands. The Beagle[2] sailed round Chatham Island, and anchored in several bays. One night I slept on shore on a part of the island, where black truncated cones were extraordinarily numerous: from one small eminence[3] I counted sixty of them, all surmounted by craters more or less perfect. The greater number consisted merely of a ring of red scoriae[4] or slags[5],

[1]**fissures** – *great cracks*
[2]**The Beagle** – *Darwin's ship*
[3]**eminence** – *area of high ground*
[4]**scoriae** – *pieces of lava with steam-holes*
[5]**slags** – *pieces of lava*

cemented together: and their height above the plain of lava was not more than from fifty to a hundred feet; none had been very lately active. The entire surface of this part of the island seems to have been permeated, like a sieve, by the subterranean vapours: here and there the lava, whilst soft, has been blown into great bubbles; and in other parts, the tops of caverns similarly formed have fallen in, leaving circular pits with steep sides. From the regular form of the many craters, they gave to the country an artificial appearance, which vividly reminded me of those parts of Staffordshire, where the great iron-foundries are most numerous. The day was glowing hot, and the scrambling over the rough surface and through the intricate thickets, was very fatiguing; but I was well repaid by the strange Cyclopean scene. As I was walking along I met two large tortoises, each of which must have weighed at least two hundred pounds: one was eating a piece of cactus, and as I approached, it stared at me and slowly walked away; the other gave a deep hiss, and drew in its head. These huge reptiles, surrounded by the black lava, the leafless shrubs, and large cacti, seemed to my fancy like some antediluvian[6] animals. The few dull-coloured birds cared no more for me than they did for the great tortoises.

From *The Journals of Charles Darwin*

[6]antediluvian – *primitive*

Looking at language

1   The reader gains an impression of the landscape described by Darwin as being extremely hostile to human beings. Read the text closely, **empathising** with Darwin as he explored and visualising the landscape as he saw it.

   a   Identify the words and phrases that suggest the heat and dryness of the landscape.

   b   Select the words and phrases that suggest how uncomfortable the environment was for people.

Explaining the ideas

2   Darwin's diary is written deliberately in a formal and impersonal style – it is a detailed record of scientific discovery, rather than a personal account. However, by reading between the lines the reader can **deduce** some personal information about Darwin.

   Copy and complete the table below:

Personal information about Darwin	Evidence from the text
Prepared to work hard in difficult conditions to collect plant specimens	
	'The volcanic island of Fernando Noronha... the only other country where I have seen a vegetation at all like this...'

Text **3**

Places worth saving

The poet Philip Larkin wrote about the ordinary and the everyday. In this poem, he records his thoughts about a way of a life and a time that is being gradually wiped out by progress and modernisation.

Going, Going

I thought it would last my time –
The sense that, beyond the town,
There would always be fields and farms,
Where the village louts could climb
Such trees as were not cut down;
I knew there'd be false alarms

In the papers about old streets
And split-level shopping, but some
Have always been left so far;
And when the old part retreats
As the bleak high-risers come
We can always escape in the car.
Things are tougher than we are, just

As earth will always respond
However we mess it about;
Chuck filth in the sea, if you must:
The tides will be clean beyond.
– But what do I feel now? Doubt?

Or age, simply? The crowd
Is young in the M1 café;
Their kids are screaming for more –
More houses, more parking allowed,
More caravan sites, more pay.
On the Business Page, a score

Of spectacled grins approve
Some takeover bid that entails
Five per cent profit (and ten
Per cent more in the estuaries): move
Your works to the unspoilt dales
(Grey area grants)! And when
You try to get near the sea
In summer …

It seems, just now,
To be happening so very fast;
Despite all the land left free
For the first time I feel somehow
That it isn't going to last,

That before I snuff it, the whole
Boiling will be bricked in
Except for the tourist parts –
First slum of Europe: a role
It won't be so hard to win,
With a cast of crooks and tarts.

And that will be England gone,
The shadows, the meadows, the lanes,
The guildhalls, the carved choirs.
There'll be books; it will linger on
In galleries; but all that remains
For us will be concrete and tyres.

Most things are never meant.
This won't be, most likely: but greeds
And garbage are too thick-strewn
To be swept up now, or invent
Excuses that make them all needs.
I just think it will happen, soon.

By Philip Larkin

What the writer thinks

1 In the first three verses of the poem, Larkin explains his reasons for thinking that the past would '*last (his) time*'. Read these verses closely, then explain:

a What were his reasons for thinking this?

b What line signals to the reader that the poet's ideas have now begun to change? What are the two reasons for this change?

c What words used by the poet suggest his contempt for the way we live now?

2 In the next three verses Larkin describes the people he sees as being responsible for what is happening. Re-read these verses and try to **see images**.

a Describe two of the groups of people he singles out as wanting '*more*'.

b How can you tell that he does not approve of them? Summarise his attitude.

c How might the sentence '*in summer…*' have ended if the poet had finished it?

3 The last three verses of the poem describe what the poet thinks '*will happen, soon.*'

a Describe three of the things he thinks will happen.

b Why do you think he uses the phrase '*before I snuff it*' rather than 'before I die?'

c Is the title of the poem appropriate? Justify your answer.

▶ Compare

You are the editor of a magazine for teenagers. One of your writers has sent you the three texts you have just read, and suggested that you include the material in an article called 'Lost places'. Before you can begin to write the article, you will have to take the idea to the editorial board and persuade them that it has relevance and appeal for a teenage audience.

1 **Re-read** the texts carefully, with a teenage audience in mind. How could each text be made relevant and interesting to a teenage audience? Prepare your ideas for the board meeting. For each text, make notes about:

• why it would appeal to teenagers
• why it would not appeal to teenagers
• ways of making it appeal to teenagers.

2 The board has accepted your ideas. Before you begin to write your article, **re-read** the three texts carefully. Pick out all the key information you want to include in your article.

3 You should now write your 'Lost places' article. Remember to prepare a brief introduction and a conclusion.

Pearson Education
Edinburgh Gate
Harlow
Essex
CM20 2JE

England and Associated Companies throughout the World

ISBN 0582 84864 4

First published 2004
Second impression 2005

Printed in China GCC/02

The Publisher's policy is to use paper manufactured from sustainable forests

Designed by Jackie Hill 320 Design

Picture Research by Ann Thomson

The cover photograph has been kindly supplied by Zefa Visual Media UK Ltd

Sources and acknowledgements

Texts

We are grateful to the following for permission to reproduce copyright material:

Pat Ashworth for an extract concerning Ellen MacArthur by Pat Ashworth originally published in *Derbyshire Life and Countryside*; Atlantic Syndication for an extract from 'Junk Food addicts may sue' by James Chapman as published on *The Daily Mail* website 14th July 2003; Avalon Management Group Ltd on behalf of Jenny Eclair for the article 'Driving Miss Daisy' as published in the *AA Magazine* summer 2003 © Jenny Eclair; Bloomsbury Publishing plc for an extract from *Kitchen Confidential* by Anthony Bourdain; Canongate Books Limited for an extract from *An Island Odyssey* by Hamish Haswell-Smith; Casarotto Ramsay & Associates Limited for an extract from *Educating Rita* © Willy Russell 1985. All rights whatsoever in this play are strictly reserved and application for performance etc, must be made before rehearsal to Casarotto Ramsay & Associates Ltd, National House, 60-66 Wardour Street, London W1V 4ND. No performance may be given unless a licence has been obtained;
David Higham Associates and Egmont Books for an extract from *The Wreck of the Zanzibar* by Michael Morpurgo; dooyoo.co.uk Ltd for an extract concerning Kefalonia published on www.dooyoo.co.uk; Dorling Kindersley for an extract from *Outdoor Survival Guide* by Hugh McManners © Hugh McManners 1998; Egmont Books and PFD on behalf of William Nicolson for an extract from *Slaves of Mastery* by William Nicholson © William Nicolson; Eland Books for an extract from *The Road to Nab End* by William Woodruff; Faber and Faber Limited for the poem 'Going, Going' by Philip Larkin; Geographical for an extract from 'In search of the true explorer' by Benedict Allen published in *Geographical* December 2002 © Geographical, the Magazine of the Royal Geographical Society; Guardian News Service Ltd for extracts from 'Food has four seasons' by Matthew Fort published in *The Guardian* 24th May 2003 © Matthew Fort, 'Jim our scans now show' by Tim Radford published in *The Guardian* 4th July 2003 © Guardian and 'Ice Cream fat stuns Scientists' by David Adam published in *The Guardian* 25th July 2003 © Guardian; HarperCollins Publishers for an extract from *City of Beasts* by Isabel Allende; Hodder and Stoughton Limited for extracts from *Bend it Like Beckham* by Narinder Dhami and *What do we know about Buddhism?* by

Anita Ganeri; Kendra Inman for an extract from 'Swimming Against the Tide' by Kendra Inman published in *The Guardian* 12th May 1999; Jodrell Bank Observatory for the advert *Explore the Universe* by Dr Tim O'Brien; Little, Brown and Company (Inc) for an extract from *Long Walk to Freedom* by Nelson Mandela © 1994, 1995 by Nelson Rolihlahla Mandela; Macmillan Publishers for an extract from *The Machine Gunners* by Robert Westall; Florence McNeil for the poem 'First Dive'; Microsoft for the advert *Unleash the wrath of the gods* from *Age of Mythology* © Microsoft Corporation; New Internationalist for an extract from 'We, the Working Children of the Third World, propose...' and 'Young Daughter of Mali' published in *New Internationalist Magazine* July 1997; New Woman Magazine for an extract from 'Diet 2000' by Judy Ridgway published in the supplement of *New Woman Magazine* November 1994; Penguin Group (UK) for extracts from *Survive! Volcanic Fury* by Jack Dillon published by Puffin © Working Partners Ltd 1999 and *Tribes* by Catherine Macphail published by Puffin © Catherine Macphail 2001; PFD on behalf of James Berry for the poem 'Hurricane' by James Berry © James Berry, and PFD for an extract from *Whose Side are you on?* by Martyn Forrester; Piccadilly Press for an extract from *Staying Cool, Surviving School* by Rosie Ruston © Rosie Rushton 1993; Scholastic Ltd and Ed Victor Limited for an extract from *Talking Point: Alien Contact* by Herbie Brennan published by Scholastic Children's Books © Herbie Brennan 1998; Simon and Schuster for an extract from *Cadbury's The Taste of Chocolate* by Patricia Dunbar; Transport 2000 for an extract concerning Walking and Cycling as published on www.transport2000.org.uk; A P Watt Ltd on behalf of the Literary Executors of the Estate of H.G. Wells for an extract from *The War of the Worlds* by H.G. Wells; World Wildlife Fund International for an extract from 'Ancient Coral Reefs under Attack' by Joanna Benn as published on www.panda.org 18th June 2003 © WWF World Wide Fund for Nature. All rights reserved; and World Wildlife Fund UK for an extract from 'How much do you care about wildlife?' © WWF 2003.

We have been unable to trace the owners of some copyright material and would appreciate any information that would enable us to do so.

Photographs

Brand X Pictures for pages 35, 36; Bruce Coleman for page 44; Cadbury's for page 116; Corbis for pages 38, 39, 42-43, 57, 67, 74, 78-79, 83 (middle), 101, 102, 103, 124, 128-129, 130, 132, 155; DK images for pages 26, 27, 32, 33 (top), 68 (top), 80 (top), 115; From The Wreck of the Zanzibar © 1995 Egmont Books Limited, 239 Kensington High Street, London, W8 6SA. Illustrations copyright © 1995 Christian Birmingham for page 41; Eye Ubiquitous/David Cumming for page 82, /Paul Seheult for page 83 (top); Getty images for pages 12 (top), 18, 19, 28, 48, 51, 63, 68 (main), 90-91, 93, 105, 110-111, 112-113, 125, 139, 152-153, 154, 158; From What Do We Know About Buddhism by Anita Ganeri. Reproduced by permission of Hodder and Stoughton Limited for page 83 (bottom); Kingfisher plc/Erik Lindkvist for page 149 (upper middle), /Thierry Martinez for pages 142,148, 149 (lower middle), 149 (bottom), 150, /Rick Tomlinson for page 149 (top); The Kobal Collection for pages 54, 120; Mary Evans Picture Library for pages 65, 122; Box Shot reprinted with permission from Microsoft Corporation for page 109; Norwegian Institute of Marine Research for page 153 (inset); Pacific Tsunami Museum Archive Photo. 1946 tsunami: Yasuki Arakaki Collection, photographer: Cecilio Licos for page 86; Page One Media for page 49; PhotoDisc for pages 33 (bottom), 37, 45, 55, 80 (bottom), 89, 127; Photolibrary.com/Richard Handwerk for page 137; Popperfoto for pages 9, 12 (bottom); Retna for pages 30, 140 (top), /Chris Beall for page 62, /John Powell for page 140 (middle), /Philip Reeson for page 31; Robert Harding Picture Library for pages 95, 96 (background), / Tom Ang for pages 15, 16-17, /Scott Barrow/Int'l Stock for page 118, /Roy Rainford for page 55, /Tony Waltham for pages 98-99 (background); Ronald Grant Archive for pages 53, 70, 96 (inset); Topham/AP for pages 24-25, /Image Works for page 61, /PA for pages 46, 157, /Photri for page 86 (bottom), /Picturepoint for pages 14, 20-21, 22, 73, 134, 135, 143, 145, /Picturepoint/UPPA for page 136; The University of Manchester/Jodrell Bank Observatory for page 108; John Walmsley for pages 10, 13; WWF-UK for page 38.

Illustrations

Jamil Akib (Illustration) pages 58-60; Dave Smith (The Organisation) page 77; Kim Williams (320 Design) page 87; Antonia Enthoven (Illustration) page 98; Sam Hadley (Artist Partners) pages 106-107; Martin Hargreaves (Illustration) page 147.